POCKET
WINE
GUIDE

Acknowledgements

The publishers wish to thank the many individuals who contributed to this guide. A special thanks is reserved for Ann, Ros, Jane and Eddy for their patient assistance in helping Christopher prepare the guide.

Designers: Design 23

Illustrations: Malcolm Porter

First published 1981 by
Octopus Books Limited
59 Grosvenor Street, London W1

This edition produced exclusively
for The Victoria Wine Company 1985

© 1981 1982 Octopus Books Limited
Revised edition 1982

ISBN 0 7064 1524 8

Produced by Mandarin Publishers Limited
22a Westlands Road,
Quarry Bay, Hong Kong

Printed in Hong Kong

Contents

Introduction

There are many wine books on bookshop shelves at the moment and there are probably as many again that have not found the publisher bold enough to invest in them. In the main, they fall into four classes, the skeletal, the lyrical, the coffee table and the specialist. The best of each have their merits. The skeletal seeks to give the maximum amount of information in the minimum amount of space; there are plenty of facts, but little opinion. The lyrical tend to dwell on the pleasures of past bottles, generally no longer available. (The reader's pleasures might not be the same as those of a reader of Playboy, but they are just as vicarious.) The coffee table book can be more or less useful, but it is an expensive way to gain information. The specialist book may appeal to someone in the wine trade, or the deeply interested layman, but it tends to be beyond the comprehension of the average interested amateur.

With this book, we have tried to take the skeleton of each major wine-producing region of the world and get it dressed by a specialist. In some cases the costumier comes from the country concerned; in some cases he has lived and worked in the trade there; in each case he is an expert. You will see that amongst the contributors, there are a number of Masters of Wine (MW). This qualification is the highest in the wine trade in Britain and its standing is now recognized throughout the world. A number of the writers have also written full-length books on their subject. Each has something special to offer.

Whilst each contributor has been given broad guidelines, each has also been encouraged to express his own opinions. Here, then, is our reason for the book. In it you should find all the basic information on the world's wines you might seek. In addition, the individual approach to each area gives much more – a feeling for wine and for the people who make it, the people who sell it and the people who drink it.

It would be interesting, though vain, to calculate how many corks have been pulled and how many glasses have been downed to provide the knowledge that has gone into this book. We hope that it has all been worthwhile.

Storing, buying and tasting

Too often when you open a bottle of what should be a great wine, you are disappointed. Whose fault is it? As often as not, it is because the wine, at some time in its life, has been badly handled. Whilst it is difficult to insist that your merchant should store his wine correctly and not keep it standing upright on his shop shelves, you always have the choice as to where you buy your wine, and you can always ask to see how it is stored.

Storing

A more relevant consideration is the way you treat your wine once you get it home. Few houses nowadays have a cellar, so where do you keep your bottles? Ideally a wine store should have a constant temperature and should not suffer in any way from vibration.

Perhaps the best temperature at which to store wine is 12°C, but as long as there is little change throughout the year, a few degrees on either side make little difference. If you do have a cellar, do not store your wine in with the central heating boiler, or even with central heating pipes, unless they are very well lagged. I do not have a cellar, but store my wine on racks in a fitted cupboard, against an inside wall in a room without central heating. Though a garage or a loft might seem suitable for storing wine, often the temperature variations are considerable during the year. It should be noted that, the warmer the place where you keep your wine, the quicker it will age and the quicker it will go off. If your cellar is slightly damp, it can help with the conservation of your wine, but it is as well to protect the labels because they will tend to come away from the bottles.

In a restaurant, do not be overpowered by the wine waiter; choose whatever wine you wish with whatever dish you wish. There is no doubt that certain wines go better with certain foods, but wine is primarily something to be enjoyed. Whilst the perfectionist may not be satisfied with anything less than perfection, most of us seek no more than pleasure from our wine. The *sommelier* should show you the bottle before he opens it. Check that it is what you have ordered; sometimes the vintage or the grower might be different and that can make a great deal of difference. He should show you the cork when he has opened the bottle. Firstly, look at the end which has been in contact with the wine. If it is dry, it suggests that the bottle has been stored upright for some time and this may have affected the quality of the wine. Smell the end of the cork; if it smells of wine, so much the better; if it smells of cork, the wine is almost certain to be tainted.

5

Serving

Should a wine be decanted or not? This is a question that has no one answer. For me, there are four main reasons for decanting. Firstly, some wines benefit from a little aeration before being served. Generally speaking, Bordeaux red wines gain from the oxidization that decanting brings; red wines from Burgundy do not. The second reason is to separate the wine from any deposit that might have formed in the bottle. The Burgundian achieves this by putting his bottle in a wine basket and pouring gently. The *Bordelais* prefers a decanter. Thirdly, a decanter is useful if you want to show the wine blind and let your guests guess what it is.

At what temperature should wine be served? Generally speaking, white wine should be served cool, red wine should be served rather warmer. Books speak of red wines being served at room temperature. Frequently in this age of central heating and open fires, this is far too warm. I am convinced that it is infinitely preferable to serve wines too cool than too warm. It is easy to warm your glass in the palm of your hands. You cannot cool a wine down once it has been served. Speaking in generalities, I would leave a bottle of white wine in the fridge for an hour before you need it, a bottle of Beaujolais in the fridge for half an hour; I would bring a bottle of red Burgundy up to the dining room an hour before the meal, and a claret three hours before. If you are not decanting the claret, draw the cork an hour or so before serving. In the end, it is only knowing each individual wine and how it has developed that you can know what is best for it. I have regularly served red Burgundies at cellar temperature and received nothing but compliments; I have just as regularly had bottles of red Burgundy that have been in restaurant dining rooms for so long that they have tasted stewed.

Ideally, a wine glass should show off a wine to its best. It should be clear, uncut crystal and tulip-shaped. It should hold in total about a third of a bottle but should be filled no more than a third full. The tulip shape enables you to swirl the wine round to release the bouquet. Whilst there are very good commercial reasons for the very large glasses you come across particularly in Burgundian restaurants – you need the second bottle more quickly – they are little more than an affectation.

Tasting

How do you taste wine? Firstly, you look at it. If it is cloudy there is either something the matter with the wine itself, or it has been badly served. In both cases, you have good grounds for sending it back. In red wines, a brown rim is a sign of age; in white wines, the colour becomes deeper.

Next, you smell it. If there is anything wrong with the wine, it is generally at this stage that it becomes fully apparent. Primarily, a wine should smell clean; if it smells fusty, then it is probably corked. (Corked does not mean that there are pieces of cork floating about in the wine; just fish these out, they will not affect the wine in any way.) If there is a smell of mould, it might have come from a dirty cask. Often it is worthwhile to smell your glass before any wine is poured into it. If it has been washed in detergent and has not been properly rinsed, the best of wines can be ruined. If you are in a restaurant and have doubts about the wine at this or any other stage, ask the wine waiter to taste it.

The time of tasting arrives. By now, you should have made up your mind as to whether the wine is drinkable or not. Most are! To get the real taste of a wine, put a little in your mouth, lean forward, purse your lips and breathe in through them. This releases the essences of the flavour. The art of tasting wines has had as many books written about it as any other facet of wine, but the important thing is to be able to store in your memory what has struck you about a particular wine. It is of little importance that you think that the wines of Vosne-Romanée taste of, perhaps, violets, whilst the person next to you finds raspberries. Each person has different taste sensations. I have heard an expert talk for half an hour about the taste of a single wine, detailing in depth each nuance as the flavour developed in his mouth.

It is important, when tasting wine, to consider for what purpose the wine was made. German wines, for example, are made for drinking by themselves, without food. Thus they are often low in alcohol and have very delicate flavours. On the other hand, many of the wines of Italy are made to accompany the local dishes, which might be rich in oil. Thus the wines are high in acidity and often coarser in taste. By themselves, they can be unattractive, but they can be ideal partners for *osso buco* or *tagliatelli alla bolognese*.

Something that can easily be recognized in red wines is tannin. This furs up your tongue and teeth. In tannin lies the future of a wine. This will disappear with age, but, in the meantime, it holds the wine together. If you are tasting wines with a view to laying them down for consumption in the far future, tannin is something for which to look.

One final thought, if you are buying wine for investment, it is essential to take into account the keeping potential of the wine, as well as its resaleability. Generally speaking, vintage port lasts the longest, then clarets, then Burgundies. Ask your wine merchant about the characteristics of each vintage before taking a decision and never pay more than you would pay for drinking it yourself. You just might have to!

France

Lar R.

Angers
Tours

Nantes
VAL-DE-LOIRE

Cher R.

MUSCADET

Bordeaux
Bergerac

BERGERAC

BORDEAUX

Garonne R.

Toulouse

Pau

JURANCON

Paris

Reims •
Epernay •
Mame R.
CHAMPAGNE

Strasbourg •

ALSACE

Colmar •

CHABLIS

ore R.

POUILLY

Saône R.

SANCERRE

BOURGOGNE

JURA

Mâcon •

BEAUJOLAIS

SAVOIE

Lyons •
Rhône R.

Dordogne R.

CAHORS

RHONE

AILLAC

Avignon •

LANGUEDOC

COTES-DE-PROVENCE

Montpellier •

Aude R.

Narbonne •

Marseilles •

ROUSSILLON

Perpignan •

9

Classification of French Wines

The consumption of wine in France is falling, but whilst the
sales of fruit juice and beer are increasing, so are those of the
better wines. How then are French wines classified?

At the bottom level are the *Vins de Table,* or everyday
drinking wines. These account for about six out of every ten
bottles produced in the country. Amongst these are the six
star returnable bottles on sale in every corner shop and the
carafe wine in every restaurant. At the top end of this class
come the *Vins de Pays.* These come from specific vineyard
regions, which might be as large as several *départements* (for
example, Vin de Pays d'Oc), from just one *département* (Vin
de Pays du Tarn), or from a much smaller area within one or
more *départements* (Vin de Pays des Coteaux de Peyriac). To
achieve this status, the wines must come from the specific
area, be made from a broad range of grape varieties that are
deemed suitable for the production of wine in the area and
undergo both tasting and analytical tests. The quantity that
may be produced in each hectare of vineyards is also limited.
The wines can be recognized by the words 'Vin de Pays' on
the label, followed by a more precise geographical description. Generally, they are made throughout the south and
southwest of France, the Rhône Valley, the Loire Valley,
Savoie, and the Jura. Because of the geographical distribution of the vineyards, there is much more red wine made than
white, and there is a broad variety of styles of wine.

The next highest classification is VDQS *(Vin Délimité de
Qualité Supérieure).* The controls are similar to those for the
Vins de Pays, but rather than being super ordinary wines,
they often have pretensions to the highest classification of all,
Appellation Contrôlée. The rules surrounding this classification stipulate which varieties of grape may be grown, the
maximum yield per hectare, the minimum alcoholic
strength of the wine, as well as details about methods of
pruning, and other viticultural techniques. AC wines are the
greatest wines of France, ranging from Bordeaux, where the
production might be a million or more hectolitres in a year,
to the tiny La Romanée vineyard in Burgundy, where the
average production is just twenty-six hectolitres, or the even
smaller Château Grillet in the Rhône Valley.

One thing should be made clear – the various classification of
French wines do not guarantee their quality, they only
guarantee their source and method of production. As a
generality, the price of a wine does not relate directly to its
intrinsic merits, but rather to supply and demand. Thus there
are often many enjoyable wines to be found at reasonable
prices amongst the Vins de Pays and VDQS wines, as
opposed to the high prices of some AC wines.

BORDEAUX

Bordeaux is the capital of the ancient province of Aquitaine and lies on a bend of the Garonne river in south-west France. The Garonne flows north-westwards from the Pyrenees towards the Atlantic Ocean, and some 10 kilometres north of Bordeaux it is joined from the east by the Dordogne river. Together these form the estuary of the Gironde. The Gironde also gives its name to the *département* in which Bordeaux lies. Virtually all the land in the Gironde *département* is authorized for making wine. This is the largest quality wine-growing area in France.

The Gironde *département* produces about 5 million hectolitres of wine a year, which is roughly 8 per cent of the total production of France. And of this output, 85 per cent of the red wine and 60 per cent of the white is Appellation Controlée, or quality wine.

This total production is approximately three times that of the whole of Burgundy or the Rhône valley, and ten times that of the combined Côte d'Or (the heartland of Burgundy) and Chablis. One Château, Pontet-Canet, the largest of the classed growths, produces 40,000 cases, more than the appellation Hermitage in the Rhône valley. The commune of St-Emilion produces 300 times more, with 2½ million cases, than the commune of Nuits St-Georges.

Classification of wines

Bordeaux is the home of large wine-growing estates (Châteaux) and it is under these single-property names that all the best wines are marketed. There are many 'Château' wines, ranging from famous names like Château Latour to an almost anonymous 'petit Château'. At various times – particularly in 1855, and for various separate regions in the 1950s – the best wines have been officially classified as

CHATEAU
FOMBRAUGE

GRAND CRU
SAINT-EMILION
APPELLATION SAINT-ÉMILION GRAND CRU CONTROLÉE
1975

Ste DE FOMBRAUGE, PROPRIÉTAIRE A St CHRISTOPHE DES BARDES GIRONDE
MISE EN BOUTEILLES AU CHATEAU
73 cl

first, second, third, fourth and fifth 'growths' (crus). These are the 'Cru Classé' wines and they are the aristocracy of the bordeaux area. Classed growths are also known as Premier Grand Cru Classé (first cru) and also Grand Cru Classé (2nd-5th cru). The Médoc has beneath these additional classifications Cru Exceptionnel, together with Cru Bourgeois Supérieur and Cru Bourgeois.

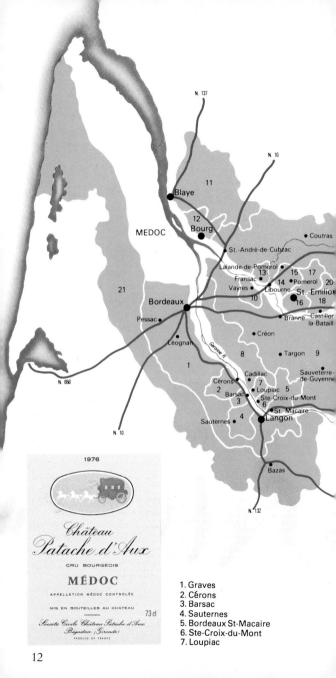

N. 137

N. 10

● Blaye

12 ● Bourg

MEDOC

11

● Coutras

St.-André-de-Cubzac ●

Lalande-de-Pomerol ●
13   15   17
Fransac ●   14   Pomerol   20
Vayres ●   Libourne ●   St.-Emilion
10   16   18

Bordeaux ●

21

Pessac ●

Léognan ●

Branne ●   Castillon
la-Bataill

● Créon

N. 650

Garonne R.

1

8   ● Targon   9

Cérons
2   Cadillac   7
Barsac   ● Loupiac   5
3   Ste-Croix-du-Mont
6
● St. Macaire
Sauternes ●   4   Langon

Sauveterre-
de-Guyenne

N. 10

N. 132

● Bazas

1976

Château
Patache d'Aux

CRU BOURGEOIS

MÉDOC

APPELLATION MÉDOC CONTROLÉE

MIS EN BOUTEILLES AU CHATEAU

73 cl

Société Civile Château Patache d'Aux
Bégadan (Gironde)

PRODUCE OF FRANCE

1. Graves
2. Cérons
3. Barsac
4. Sauternes
5. Bordeaux St-Macaire
6. Ste-Croix-du-Mont
7. Loupiac

12

8. 1^{eres} Côtes de Bordeaux
9. Entre Deux Mers
10. Graves de Vayres
11. Blayais
12. Bourgeais
13. Fronsac Canon-Fronsac
14. Pomerol
15. Lalande de Pomerol
16. St-Emilion
    St-Georges St-Emilion
    Montagne St-Emilion
17. Lussac St-Emilion
    Puisseguin St-Emilion
18. Côtes de Castillon
19. Ste-Foy Bordeaux
20. Bordeaux Côtes de Francs
21. Bordeaux

Many types of wine are produced in the Bordeaux area. The reds are called claret, and, in general, come from north of Bordeaux, in the Médoc and Haut-Médoc; from near the town of Libourne on the north bank of Dordogne, in the appellations of St-Emilion and its surrounding communes, Pomerol and Fronsac; and from the east bank of the Gironde in Blaye and Bourg.

The white wines of Bordeaux range from very dry to very sweet. The sweetest luscious wines come from Sauternes, a region which includes Barsac. Less sweet wines come from neighbouring Cérons, Loupiac, and Ste-Croix-du-Mont. Cheaper, dry wines come from the Entre-Deux-Mers. The Graves produces whites which vary in style and quality and can be dry to medium, and some red wine, particularly from those vineyards nearer to Bordeaux.

Climate, Landscape and Soil

The climate of the Bordeaux area is dominated by the nearby Atlantic Ocean. In general, it is warm, temperate, sufficiently hot to mature red grapes successfully (red grapes require more sun than white), but not too dry or hot to bake them.

Winters are mild, with few severe frosts and only a suggestion of snow. Summers are hot but tempered periodically by rain. Autumns are moist and misty.

The Gironde on the whole is dull and flat country. East of the city of Bordeaux, across the river into the Entre-Deux-Mers, or further over in the Blayais and Bourgais, the countryside is green, quite lush and rolling, while south and west of the city lie the Landes, mile upon mile of coniferous trees planted in sandy soil or marsh. To the north is the Médoc, an almost flat land of sand and gravel.

The best wine comes from vines grown in a poor soil – that is, a soil deficient in humus and nitrogenous products. For this reason certain parts of the more alluvial land next to the Gironde estuary are not authorized for making appellation Bordeaux wine. These stretches of land are known as the *palus*.

The best wine-making land here consists of four elements: gravel, sand, clay and limestone. Gravel is particularly found in the Médoc and the Graves, and on the Pomerol/St-Emilion boundary. Deep beds of gravel drain and aerate well, so the roots of the vine can probe deep for water and nutrients, producing a wine of great depth of quality. Sand adds acidity and finesse to the wine. Clay will produce full-bodied wines, well-coloured, rich and robust, perhaps coarse. Limestone produces wine with a lack of body but with a pronounced bouquet and alcohol content. When mixed with clay and gravel, as it is in the Graves and the Sauternes, it is an excellent soil for the making of white wines. The same soil, rich in iron, and on a harder limestone-rock base, produces the rich, warm red wines of St-Emilion.

Grape varieties

Red grapes Unlike most other fine wines, red Bordeaux is made from a mixture of grapes with complementary characteristics. From the Cabernet grapes come body, colour and backbone, from the Merlot come softness, suppleness and fruit. Cabernet wines take longer to mature but last longer; with Merlot the opposite is the case. So different combinations of grapes will considerably alter the style of the resulting wine, which explains the change in character between a Médoc and a wine of St-Emilion or Pomerol.

CABERNET SAUVIGNON, the most important Bordeaux grape, is grown all over the world. The berries themselves are small and tightly packed together on the bunch. They develop late, are resistant to disease and produce a wine of good colour, with body and tannin, and with an initial hardness or firmness which requires some years to soften. Cabernet Sauvignon, the main grape of the Médoc region, gives its finer wines their finesse and blackcurrant flavour.

CABERNET FRANC produces a wine similar to Cabernet Sauvignon but with less backbone and distinction. The grapes themselves are slightly larger, and less tightly packed together. In wine production they contribute sugar and alcohol and add to the volume. The grape is grown throughout the Bordeaux region – in the Médoc it is a junior partner to the Cabernet Sauvignon, and in St-Emilion, where it is known as the Bouchet, it is used with the Merlot.

MERLOT develops sooner than the Cabernets, and the berries are larger and looser in the bunch. It produces a soft, round wine without a lot of tannin or body, and with a sweeter, somewhat spicier flavour: 'fruit-cake' is a common description. This grape contributes the fruit and the delicacy, and matures more quickly than Cabernet. Merlot is widely grown throughout the region, and is the predominant grape in St-Emilion and Pomerol.

MALBEC produces a large quantity of big grapes, and the wine that comes from them is soft and forward but of less style than Merlot. It is grown in the lesser areas and in St-Emilion and Pomerol, where it is known as the Pressac.

PETIT VERDOT is hardly seen any more except in a few top Médoc properties, because it is difficult to grow and prone to disease. It produces a small quantity of wine of fine colour, backbone and acidity, which needs time to mature.

CARMENERE is authorized but has now practically disappeared. It is similar to the Cabernet.

White grapes White Bordeaux is also usually produced from a blend of grapes.

SAUVIGNON, the most important, has nothing to do with the Cabernet Sauvignon. It is a good producer and is resistant to disease. The wine it produces is fresh, with balanced acidity but without a great deal of body, and has a pronounced flavour of redcurrants or gooseberries. It is predominant in the *encépagement* (proportion of grape varieties used) for dry white wines. It is used on its own for some inexpensive wines, which are best drunk young.

SEMILLON produces a softer, richer, fatter wine with less acidity than the Sauvignon. It is prone to disease, both *pourriture grise* (grey rot) and *pourriture noble* (noble rot) and so is widely grown in those areas such as Sauternes and Barsac where this condition is needed to produce sweet wine.

MUSCADELLE, a variety of the Muscat family, is also authorized, but may only be used in small quantities as its aroma is pronounced and penetrating.

15

Proportions of Grape Varieties used
Médoc and Graves
A typical top vineyard could be planted with 55 per cent Cabernet Sauvignon, 20 per cent Cabernet Franc and 25 per cent Merlot.

St-Emilion and Pomerol
Here the proportions might be 60 per cent Merlot, 30 per cent Bouchet (Cabernet Franc) and 10 per cent Pressac (Malbec).

Graves
A top dry Graves property will be planted with 60 per cent Sauvignon and 40 per cent Semillon.

Sauternes and Barsac
The proportions will be 80 per cent Semillon, 20 per cent Sauvignon, or possibly a few per cent of Muscadelle.

The wines
The best red wines of Bordeaux are those of the Haut-Médoc and the Graves and those of St-Emilion and Pomerol. Minor red wines come from the Médoc (or Bas Médoc); from the lesser communes adjacent to St-Emilion and Pomerol; from Fronsac, Bourg and Blaye; and from the Premières Côtes de Bordeaux, and elsewhere. The best white wines come from the Sauternes and from the Graves. Others come from the Entre-Deux-Mers, and the Premières Côtes.

Haut-Médoc and Médoc
The vine-growing region of the Médoc is the eastern, Gironde-coastal part, a strip of land about 75 kilometres long by 10-15 kilometres wide. The southern half of this section, beginning just north of St-Estèphe, is the Haut-Médoc, home of the famous names of the wine châteaux.

In the coastal communes along the D2 route are some of the best-known classed-growth properties.

Ludon Home of the most southerly classed growth, Château La Lagune, a Troisième Cru which has a high reputation but few other properties of note.

Macau Notable for the fifth-growth Château Cantemerle.

Labarde The large, well-known Château Giscours heads the list, followed by Château Dauzac, a fifth growth, and Château Siran, a good Bourgeois Supérieur.

Arsac This commune, inland from Labarde, has one classed growth, Château du Tertre.

Cantenac One of the most important communes, containing Châteaux Brane-Cantenac, Palmer, Issan, Prieuré-Lichine, Cantenac-Brown, Boyd-Cantenac, Kirwan, and Poujet, all classed growths, and Château d'Angludet, a popular Cru Exceptionnel.

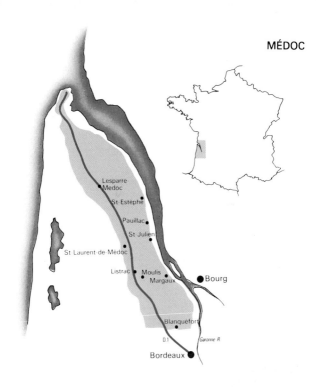

Margaux Home of Château Margaux itself, together with Châteaux Rauzan-Gassies, Rausan-Ségla, Durfort-Vivens, Lascombes, Malescot, Marquis de Terme, Marquis d'Alesme Becker, and Ferrière. These are all classed growths.

Soussans No classed growths, but contains the Cru Exceptionnel Château Bel Air Marquis de Ligré and the Bourgeois Supérieurs Château La Tour du Mons, Château Labégorce, Château Labégorce-Zédé and Château l'Abbé Gorsse de Gorsse.

The last five communes, in whole or in part, can take the appellation Margaux otherwise the wines are Haut Médoc.

Avensan, Arcins, Lamarque, Cussac These communes lie between Soussans and St-Julien. They have no classed

17

growths, but a few well-known Bourgeois Supérieurs such as Château Lanessan, Château Citran, and Château Paveil de Luze. The appellation is Haut Médoc.

Moulis, Listrac These two inland communes lie behind and to the north of Margaux. Moulis has a number of good Bourgeois Supérieur properties with variations on the name Poujeaux, as well as the excellent Château Chasse-Spleen. Listrac's top wines are Châteaux Fonréaud, Fourcas Hosten and Fourcas Dupré.

St-Laurent This commune, which lies behind St-Julien, contains three classed growths, La Tour Carnet, Belgrave and Camensac, and an important Bourgeois Supérieur, Châteaux Caronne Ste-Gemme. Appellation Contrôlée – Haut Médoc.

St-Julien An important coastal commune with very good classed growths: the Léovilles-Lascases, Poyferré and Barton, Ducru Beaucauillou, Gruaud-Larose, Langoa-Barton, Beychevelle, St-Pierre-Sevaistre, and Talbot. Good lesser growths include Châteaux Gloria, du Glana and Hortevie.

Pauillac Immediately to the north of St-Julien, Pauillac contains three Premiers Crus: Lafite, Latour and Mouton Rothschild; two seconds, Pichons-Lalande and Baron; a fourth growth, Château Duhart Milon; and a number of fifths, Batailley, Haut-Batailley, Lynch-Bages, Pontet Canet, Grand-Puy-Lacoste, Grand-Puy-Ducasse, Lynch-Moussas, Clerc-Milon-Mendon, Mouton-Baronne-Philippe, Pédesclaux, Haut-Bages-Libéral, and Croizet-Bages. There are a number of good Bourgeois growths, including Haut-Bages-Montpelou, Fonbadet and Pibran, and a well-established co-operative which sells its wine as La Rose Pauillac.

St-Estèphe This commune, immediately to the north of Pauillac, has five classed growths: Cos D'Estournel, Montrose, Calon Ségur, Lafon Rochet and Cos Labory; and a large number of excellent Bourgeois growths, including Châteaux de Pez, Ormes de Pez, Phélan Segur, and Meyney.

St-Sauveur, Cissac, Vertheuil, St-Seurin These are the four remaining important communes of the Haut Médoc, forming a ring round the back of Pauillac and St-Estèphe. They have no classed growths but some good Bourgeois Supérieurs, including Châteaux Liversan, Ramage la Batisse, Cissac, le Bourdieu, Verdignan, and Coufran.

Haut-Médoc wines, with their high proportion of Cabernet Sauvignon, and the influence of new oak in which they have been matured, are well coloured, full, firm and oaky in character – tannic and austere when young, rich and aristocratic when old. Of all of these, the fullest and richest came from the communes of Pauillac and St-Julien. St-Estèphe wines, like those from the inland communes of Listrac and Moulis, are also full-bodied, but less tightly-knit, and with less of the classic blackcurrant taste of the Cabernet grape. The wines of Margaux are softer but silky and very elegant.

With one exception (Château Haut-Brion in the Graves), all the sixty classed growths classified in 1855 are found in the Haut-Médoc. These lie chiefly in the four communes nearest to the river: St-Estèphe to the north, then Pauillac and St-Julien and Margaux in the south. In good vintages a classed growth wine will need ten years to mature, and will keep for twenty-five years or more. The next best wines, Crus Exceptionnels and the Crus Bourgeois Supérieurs are still of very high quality, and may require five years before coming round.

The Médoc, once known as the Bas-Médoc lies north of the Haut-Médoc. Here the wines are of similar style but less good quality, though some excellent value can be found. The best wines of the Médoc are the Crus Bourgeois, which require four or five years to mature in a good vintage.

Just over the border at St-Seurin is the Gilbey property, Château Loudenne. Many useful wines are produced in the vineyards here and further north. Well-known names include Châteaux La Tour de By, Potensac, la Cardonne, St-Christoly, Patache d'Aux, La Tour St-Bonnet, and Livran.

St-Emilion and Pomerol

The communes of St-Emilion, Pomerol and their lesser neighbours lie some 40 kilometres east of Bordeaux on the north bank of the Dordogne, near the town of Libourne. This is slightly more interesting countryside than the Médoc, especially round the old town of St-Emilion itself.

The St-Emilion district has two distinct areas. Around the town, mainly on the southern facing slopes which descend abruptly to the valley, is the 'Côtes' St-Emilion, home of all but two of the Premier Grand Crus Classés. These form a ribbon immediately outside the town. Further west, adjacent to the best vineyards of Pomerol, lies the 'Graves' St-Emilion.

St-Emilion 'Côtes' The best properties, many of them far smaller than their counterparts in the Médoc, are Ausone, Château Beauséjour, Belair, Canon, Gaffelière, Magdelaine, Pavie, Trottevieille, and Clos Fourtet. Among the Grands Crus Classés, of which some sixty are listed, the following stand out: L'Angélus, Balestard la Tonnelle,

Canon-La-Gaffelière, Larcis Ducasse, Curé Bon-la-Madelaine, Fonroque, Fonplegade, and Troplong-Mondot.

St-Emilion 'Graves' This smaller area contains the outstanding Château Cheval Blanc, the Premier Cru Château Figeac, and Grands Crus Classés, La Dominique, Grand Corbin Despagne, Croque-Michotte and Grand-Barrail-Lamarzelle Figeac.

Pomerol The wines of Pomerol have never been officially classified, yet the finest wine is indisputably Château Pétrus. Among the lesser Premiers Crus, comparable with the Premiers Crus of St-Emilion, must be put Vieux Château Certan, Trotanoy, La Fleur-Pétrus, Evangile, Conseillante, Petit Village, Gazin, Latour-à-Pomerol, and Château Nenin. Lesser wines of note include Clos René, Château Plince, Château la Pointe, Château La-Grave-Trigant-de-Boisset, and Château de Sales. Many of the properties are very small and their excellent wines are not widely seen.

St-Emilion and Pomerol wines can be divided into two types. Those from the slopes around the town of St-Emilion are full and rich, aromatic and spicy, with the fruit-cake flavour of the predominant Merlot grape. They are more immediately accessible than those of the Médoc, lacking their backbone and concentration, but being round and ample, warm and fruity. The St-Emilion wines from the 'Graves' area are similar to their neighbours over the Pomerol border, and are richer still and more concentrated, plummy rather than fruit-cakey, and less loose-knit than the 'Côtes' St-Emilions.

A good St-Emilion or Pomerol, one of the dozen St-Emilion Premiers Crus and their Pomerol equivalents, will take six or seven years to mature in a good vintage and will keep for at least a further ten.

The Lesser Red Wines of Bordeaux

Lesser St-Emilion Wines Around St-Emilion, particularly to the north, are subsidiary communes, each of which add the names St-Emilion to their own. There are six of these: St-Georges, Montagne, Lussac, Puisseguin, Parsac, and the district of Sables.

Pomerol's Neighbours Pomerol has the town of Libourne on its south, the communes of Lalande-de-Pomerol and Néac to the north, and Fronsac across the palus land of the river Isle to the west.

Fronsac Fronsac, a large hill overlooking a bend of the river Dordogne, consists of two wine-making communes; nearest to the river is Côtes Canon Fronsac, named after the most famous growth; behind is Côtes Fronsac. This is a flourishing area with many excellent and reasonably priced wines made.

Bourg and Blaye The undulating countryside of Bourg and Blaye lies to the east of the Dordogne estuary, opposite the Médoc. They contain a number of properties, few of them very large compared with the classed growths on the opposite bank. They make red and a little white wine.

These districts produce wines of similar but lesser character to Pomerol and St-Emilion. They also mature sooner.

The Côtes de Bourg, the Côtes de Blaye and the Premières Côtes de Blaye produce large quantities of mainly red wine of varying but never exceptional style, usually somewhat more robust and short-lived than the wine from the classic areas. These are good sources for minor single-property wines, the 'Petits Chateaux' as they are known, which are ready for drinking within three or five years after a good vintage, sooner in a lesser year.

All Bordeaux reds, of whatever pretension to quality, will be firmer, more tannic, possibly more oaky and certainly more 'difficult' to mentally appreciate than the softer, round, slightly sweeter wines of Burgundy, or the light and very fruity wines of Beaujolais. In general, claret needs more time to mature, but it keeps the longest of all red wines.

The Graves
The Graves begins a few kilometres north of Bordeaux and runs south, round the city, down to the town of Langon, encircling the small districts of Sauternes and Cérons. Red and white wine are produced here.

The important communes of the Graves are:

Pessac and Talence Now almost engulfed by the sprawling suburbs to the west of the city, only the best properties have survived. The Premier Cru Château Haut-Brion produces red wine and a few casks of white wine. Its neighbour, Château La Mission Haut-Brion, produces a white wine under the name Château Laville-Haut-Brion, and this is perhaps the best dry white Graves. The proprietors also own Chateau La Tour-Haut-Brion. Château Pape-Clément, commemorating the name of the mediaeval pope who removed the papacy from Rome to Avignon, lies nearby.

Léognan About 20 kilometres south-west of Bordeaux and on the edge of the pine forests of the landes, this commune contains six of Graves' thirteen classified red wine properties, most of which also produce white wine. Domaine de Chevalier and Château Haut-Bailly have the best reputation: the former produces an outstanding white wine as well as its red, while the latter produces red only. The large Château Carbonnieux, and Château Fieuzal, Olivier and Malartic-Lagravière are the other four.

Cadaujac and Martillac These communes lie between Leognan and the river Garonne. Cadaujac contains the classed growth Château Bouscaut, and Martillac has Château La-Tour-Martillac and Château Smith-Haut-Lafite.

The red wines of the Graves are somewhat similar to those of Margaux in the Haut-Médoc, but they have a slight aromatic earthiness in their taste. Graves wines, with one or two exceptions, are more loosely-knit than Médocs, with a soft, oaky, sometimes roast-chestnutty flavour and a warmth rather than a firm austerity on the finish. The best, the thirteen Crus Classés, classed in 1953 and reclassified in 1959, need eight to ten years to mature after a good vintage, and will keep for at least twenty. The 'lesser' Graves red wines, with which can be coupled the reds from the Premieres Côtes de Bordeaux and the increasing number of reds of the Entre-Deux-Mers on the opposite bank of the Garonne, can vary from smaller examples of the best wines to light, very fruity wines made by modern methods for almost immediate drinking.

The best dry white wines of Bordeaux come from the Graves, mainly from the same properties that produce the best reds. Here the wines are matured in oak, and not bottled until a year or a year-and-a-half after the vintage. There is also more Sémillon in the blend than in the lesser white wines. The result is full, dry but rich and ripe, and with an underlying oakiness which reminds one of the best wines of

Burgundy. The production of wine at the very top level of quality is small, but there are a number of other properties which produce larger quantities of wine which can be extremely good, and, because at present unfashionable, very good value.

The lesser dry white wines of Bordeaux

Wine labelled simply Entre-Deux-Mers will be dry and white, as will that labelled, Bordeaux Blanc (Sec). Graves will also be dry, but Graves Supérieur will be medium. There is currently a trend in Bordeaux to bottle the dry whites in green bottles, saving the traditional clear Bordeaux white wine bottle for the sweeter wines.

The lesser 'Château' white wines of Bordeaux, whether they come from the Graves, the Entre-Deux-Mers or from the single properties in Premières Côtes, vary enormously in style and quality. In the past, and regrettably all too often even now, they have been coarse and heavy in style, with all their character buried under quantities of sulphur, a chemical used universally in wine growing areas as an anti-oxidant and disinfectant (and if used properly doing nothing but good). The best, made and looked after by modern methods and techniques, are normally light, dry and crisp, and are made largely if not exclusively from the Sauvignon grape. They will be ready for drinking within a year of the vintage and should be drunk early. Today, these wines represent excellent value.

Sauternes

Sauternes, some 40 kilometres south of Bordeaux on the west bank of the river Garonne, consists of five communes – Sauternes, Fargues, Bommes, Preignac and Barsac – and the vineyards were officially classified in 1855. Each of these properties occupies its own little mound, or 'croupe', a few metres above the surrounding countryside.

The finest Sauternes is the only 'Grand Premier Cru', Château Yquem, appropriately enough in the commune of Sauternes itself. Nearby – for this is a small region, only some 10 by 5 kilometres – are the eleven Premiers Crus, Château Rieussec in Fargues, Château Suduiraut in Preignac, and Châteaux La Tour Blanche, Lafaurie-Peyraguey, Clos-Haut-Peyraguey, Rayne-Vigneau, Rabaud-Promis, and Sigalas-Rabaud in Bommes. In the commune of Barsac are the excellent Châteaux Coutet and Climens.

Among the thirteen second growths one could perhaps single out Château Doisy-Daëne in Barsac, a property which also produces a dry wine, particularly in the less good vintages. This practice is now widely adopted in the region.

The wine of Sauternes is one of the greatest sweet wines of the world. In the autumn the grapes are left on the vines after the normal harvest date, and if the weather is humid but sunny, they will be attacked by a beneficial fungus known as *botrytis cinerea,* whose spores will evaporate the water in the grape and cause it to shrivel up. These over-ripe 'nobly' rotten grapes are carefully selected and produce a juice or must of such concentration of sugar that the resultant wine will be naturally sweet. It is also very rich and luscious, and high in glycerine, with a particular spicy tang imparted by the action of the fungus. Though extremely sweet, the acidity level is also high, and the wine, though full and rich, is not cloying and will keep for years.

The fine autumns necessary to produce good Sauternes are infrequent, and few years and few properties can produce wine with the classic *pourriture noble* Sauternes taste. Most Sauternes therefore is merely sweet, but balanced by acidity, and ready within three or four years of the vintage.

The Barsac commune has become known in its own right rather than as a part of Sauternes. In general its wines are leaner, less rich than those of the other communes, though the difference is marginal.

The lesser sweet white wines of Bordeaux

The lesser sweet wine communes – Cérons, adjacent to Barsac, and Loupiac and Ste-Croix-du-Mont on the opposite bank of the Garonne river – produce medium sweet wines of varying body and concentration depending on the property and the year. Only very rarely do these have the additional *pourriture noble* taste.

The Premières Côtes de Bordeaux produces a generic medium sweet wine, and wine labelled as such will always be medium sweet.

Rosé

Very little Bordeaux wine is produced as rosé. What there is will normally be found under the generic Bordeaux label or some brand name. It will be dry, with some fruit, similar to the very driest versions of Cabernet Rosé d'Anjou, and generally without a great deal of character or quality.

Sparkling wines

The Bordeaux area produces a quantity of sparkling wine, largely from grapes imported from other regions, and the wine is sold under a brand name rather than as Bordeaux. The most familiar is Veuve du Vernay, which comes in a fairly dry and a fairly sweet version, and is made by the 'Cuvé close' method.

Vintages

1980
Small production owing to poor flowering, especially of the Merlot grapes. Poor to average quality, better in the Médoc than in St-Emilion. Early-maturing wines.

1979
Very large harvest; average to good wines – the best of the reds will come from St-Emilion and Pomerol. Will be ready for drinking before the 1978s.

1978
Good-sized harvest and wines of good to excellent quality in both red and dry white. Some light, elegant Sauternes.

1977
Small crop, indifferent vintage.

1976
Large quantity, good quality, ample, generous, fruity wines; the best reds come from St-Julien and Pauillac. Good dry white Graves, and a good year for Sauternes. The wines should be drunk before the 1975.

1975
Fairly small crop, excellent quality, firm, full, long-lasting red wines. Fine dry wines, and firm well-balanced Sauternes. Will need a long time to mature.

1974
Very large harvest. The reds have some body but lack fruit and so are a bit ungenerous. Whites equally lack charm. Ready now.

1973
Very large harvest. The wines are soft, round and fruity, but in general are a bit weak. Some Sauternes. Ready now.

1972
Fairly small production. Poor quality.

1971
Small crop. Variable quality but some very good wines which have evolved more quickly than originally expected. Some very good wines in St-Emilion and Pomerol and good, elegant Sauternes. Ready now.

1970
Good for both quality and quantity. Attractive fruity wines with plenty of depth, consistent throughout the region, red, dry and sweet white. Ready but will keep well.

Previous good vintages for red wine 1967, 1966, 1964, 1962, 1961 (outstanding), 1959, 1955, 1953, 1952, 1949, 1948, 1947, 1945.

BURGUNDY

Burgundy has a reputation all of its own – it is the country of fine food and fine wines. The land is rich: it produces the best chickens in the world in the Bresse, the fine beef of Charolais; the rivers produce pike and tench, eel and chub, for the world renowned *pochouse*; there are frogs and snails, hams and cheeses. The wines, though, owe their reputation, in the main, to a narrow strip of infertile hillside where nothing but the vine can grow. Like many of the world's greatest wines, Burgundy is produced near the northern limit for growing the vines; low yielding grape varieties fight a constant battle with the weather. When they win they produce dry white wines without equal in the world and full-bodied red wines rivalled only by those of Bordeaux.

To find the vineyards of Burgundy you take the Autoroute du Soleil, the A6 motorway south-west from Paris; after about 160 kilometres you see an exit marked Chablis. This is the northern outpost of the vineyards; after another 130 kilometres the road crosses the col of Bessey-en-Chaume and sweeps down on the vineyards of Savigny and Beaune. This is the heart of the great vineyards of Burgundy, those of the Côte d'Or. To the south come the areas of Mercurey, the Mâconnais and Beaujolais, but Beaune is the heart and the soul of Burgundy.

Burgundy is an area of small vineyards, often split among many owners as a result of the Napoleonic laws of inheritance. The most outstanding example of this is the vineyard of Clos de Vougeot; admittedly, it is about 50 hectares in size, but there are seventy-seven different owners, of whom no less than twenty-six have little more than a nominal number of vines. Figures show that the average vineyard holding per grower throughout Burgundy is about half a hectare but these figures include even 'garden' vineplantings and they are also distorted by the Burgundian peasant's natural desire to hide as much from the tax-man as possible. In order to achieve this, he shows a number of different owners in his family for his vines, though they are worked as an entity.

The grower in Burgundy has traditionally been just that; he picked the grapes and fermented the wine, then sold it in bulk to the *négociant,* or merchant. The *négociant* aged it in cask and bottle and sold it on, in France or abroad. Recently, though, there has been a distinct move towards the grower bottling the wine himself and selling it to the restaurant or the private individual. These 'farm-gate' sales now account for about 30 per cent of the trade of Burgundy and the figures seem to have settled at this level.

The role of *négociant* is important because only he is capable of assembling large enough quantities of wine to enable serious

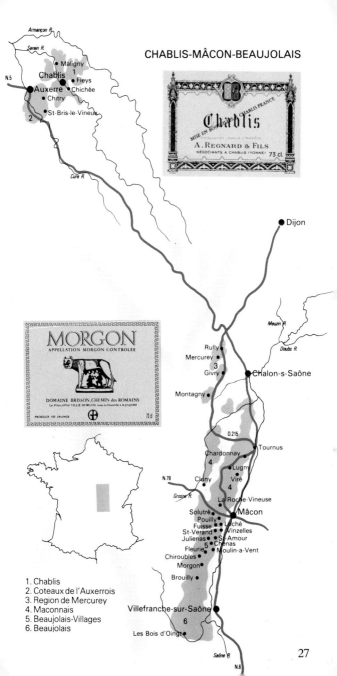

CHABLIS-MÂCON-BEAUJOLAIS

Armançon R.

Serein R.

N.5

• Maligny

Chablis **1**

• Fleys

• Chichée

Auxerre

• Chitry

2

• St-Bris-le-Vineux

Cure R.

Chablis

MISE EN BOU... ...CHABLIS FRANCE

APPELLATION CHABLIS CONTROLÉE

A. REGNARD & FILS

NÉGOCIANTS A CHABLIS (YONNE) 73 cl.

• Dijon

Meuzin R.

Doubs R.

Rully •

Mercurey •

3

Givry •

● Chalon-s-Saône

Montagny •

MORGON

APPELLATION MORGON CONTROLEE

DOMAINE BRISSON, CHEMIN des ROMAINS

Les Frères ... VILLIE-MORGON, mise en bouteille à la propriété

PRODUCE OF FRANCE   73 cl

D.215

● Tournus

Chardonnay •

4

• Lugny

N.79

Cluny •

Viré •

Grosne R.

4

La-Roche-Vineuse

Solutré •

Mâcon

Pouilly •

Loché •

Fuissé •

Vinzelles •

St-Verand •

St-Amour •

Julienas •

5

Chénas •

Fleurie •

Moulin-a-Vent •

Chiroubles •

Morgon •

Brouilly •

Villefranche-sur-Saône ●

6

Les Bois d'Oingt •

Saône R.

N.6

1. Chablis
2. Coteaux de l'Auxerrois
3. Region de Mercurey
4. Maconnais
5. Beaujolais-Villages
6. Beaujolais

27

marketing efforts to be made. Because of the multiplicity of growers, the merchant buys from a number of sources and blends within each appellation, to enable himself to have adequate quantities of wine of a standard quality. Between the grower and the merchant comes the *courtier,* or broker, who knows all the growers, what wine they have available for sale and what price they want for it. He also knows what the merchant is looking for and what price he is prepared to pay. His role is necessary in the fragmented state of the market.

Though the grower is usually separate from the shipper, many of the largest domains belong to the merchant houses. Currently almost 20 per cent of the vineyard area of the Côte d'Or is under their control and of the eight largest holdings, only two – those of Clair-Däu and the Hospices de Beaune – are independent.

Classification of wines

There are four classifications of the wines of Burgundy: at the top are the Grands Crus, of which there are eight in the Chablis area and twenty-nine on the Côte d'Or. Except in Chablis, the vineyard titles appear on their own, without giving the village name:

for example, Richebourg. Next come the Premiers Crus, of which there are already a host, and the number is slowly increasing. Confusingly, depending on its exposure on a slope, only part of a vineyard may be classified as Premier Cru. On

a label, the name of the Premier Cru vineyard appears in the same size type as the name of the village – Savigny Dominode, Nuits les Pruliers. If the vineyard is of a lower classification than Premier Cru, the vineyard name must be in smaller print than

that of the village – VOLNAY Jouères. After these come the commune appellations, which are generally labelled as the name of a village such as Meursault or Fixin, with possibly a vineyard name. Or there might be a group of villages, such as Côte de Beaune Villages.

The last classification is that of the generic *appellations,* which might cover the whole of Burgundy, such as Bourgogne Grand Ordinaire, or Bourgogne Aligoté; or a particular section, like Beaujolais or Macon Villages. It should be noted that the word Bourgogne on a label by itself, though it is a generic appellation, already denotes wine of a certain class, for it has to be made from the best grape varieties grown in that area.

As well as the geographical restrictions that control the name of each wine of Burgundy, there are also strict controls on the grape varieties used, the methods of pruning the vines, the quantity produced per acre and the method of vinification. The regulations stipulate that each wine will have to be tasted blind by an independent panel of experts before it is given the Appellation Contrôlée status.

Grape varieties

There are four main grape varieties in Burgundy: two for red wines, the Pinot Noir and the Gamay; and two for white wines, the Chardonnay and the Aligoté.

PINOT NOIR produces all the really great red wines of Burgundy.

GAMAY reaches the peak of its quality in the Beaujolais, where it makes grapey, gulping wines. A mixture of the two grape varieties, with at least a third of the former, makes a wine called Bourgogne Passetousgrains; in all but the best years this tends to be little more than ordinary and rather too high in acidity for most people's palates.

CHARDONNAY is a grape that succeeds well in a number of places, from California to New Zealand. It is used for all the best white wines of Burgundy, from Chablis in the north to Pouilly-Fuisse in the south.

ALIGOTÉ, on the other hand, is largely used for the production of Bourgogne Aligoté, a crisp, dry wine that is often mixed with Crême de Cassis, the Burgundian speciality liqueur made from blackcurrants. This cocktail is called a kir.

The wines

There are five main regions in Burgundy: Chablis, the Côte d'Or (which in turn is split into the Côte de Nuits and the Côte de Beaune), the Region de Mercurey, the Mâconnais, and the Beaujolais. Let us look at each of them and their wines in turn. In each case, I will give the names of all the Grand Cru vineyards and the names of the most common Premiers Crus.

CHABLIS

The area under vines is only a very small proportion of what it used to be as the vineyards were largely not replanted after the phylloxera blight in the 1870's and 1880's. The area suffers seriously from spring frosts and many complete vintages were destroyed. Paris is not far away and the high wages offered by the burgeoning industrial revolution proved to be an important attraction. Over the past few years, however, there has been considerable reinvestment in vineyard planting and anti-frost protection. As a result production is increasing considerably.

A typical Chablis should be crisp and with a pronounced, though not excessive, acidity. It is the traditional accompaniment for oysters. A good Grand Cru wine should not be drunk under about eight years old. The lesser qualities can be drunk correspondingly younger.

Grand Cru Bougros, les Preuses, Vaudésir, Valmur, Grenouilles, les Clos (my favourite), Blanchots, Moutonne.

Premier Cru Fourchaume, Montée de Tonnerre, Monts de Milieu, Vaucoupin, Les Fourneaux, Beauroy, Côte de Léchet, Vaillons, Melinots, Montmains.

Chablis is made from the Chardonnay grape on soil which takes its name, Kimmeridgean clay, from the small Dorset village of Kimmeridge. Petit Chablis is a wine made from peripheral vineyards on less suitable soil. It should be drunk young and is probably at its best when it is six months old. There is also an interesting wine made from the Sauvignon grape, which is much more a native of Bordeaux and the Loire; this is the Sauvignon de Saint Bris. There is a little excellent red wine made in the region, particularly in the villages of Irancy and Coulanges la Vineuse, and the Clos de la Chainette at Auxerre regularly wins awards for its rosé wines. This vineyard belongs to the local psychiatric hospital and the patients tend the vines!

Growers Robert Vocoret, Laroche, Jouchère, Long-Depaquit.

Shippers Bacheroy-Josselin, Moreau, Regnard.
Co-operative la Chablisienne.

CÔTE DE NUITS

The vineyards of the Côte d'Or used to start at the gates of Dijon, but the expanding needs of the city have forced them back some 8 kilometres. The Côte de Nuits is famous particularly for its great red wines. Any white wine that is made relies largely on its novelty to sell it. The greatest wines of the Côte go well with game, all red meats and strong cheeses. They last well and, because demand outstrips the very limited supply, have become very expensive.

Marsannay Renowned for its rosé wines, the best of Burgundy. These are made from the Pinot Noir grape and are best drunk at about eighteen months old.

Grower Clair-Däu. A good co-operative cellar.

Fixin Good to great red wines.

Premiers Crus les Arvelets, les Hervelets, la Perrière, Clos Napoléon.

Growers Pierre Gelin, Dr Marion.

Gevrey-Chambertin The reputation of the wines of this village has meant that, in some cases, quantity has become more important to the growers than quality. It has a broad range of Grands Crus and some excellent Premiers Crus.

Grands Crus Chambertin, Chambertin Clos de Bèze, Latricières-Chambertin, Charmes-Chambertin (or Mazoyères-Chambertin), Griotte-Chambertin, Mazys- (or Mazis- or Mazy-) Chambertin, Chapelle-Chambertin, Ruchottes-Chambertin.

Premiers Crus Véroilles (or Varoilles), Cazetiers, Clos Saint Jacques, Combe aux Moines, Eternelles (or Estournelles), Champitonnois (or Petite-Chapelle).
Growers Drouhin-Laroze, Armand Rousseau, Dujac, Damoy, Trapet, Camus, Louis Latour, Joseph Drouhin.

Morey-Saint Denis For long the wines of this village were under-valued, partly because traditionally they were often sold as Gevrey or Chambolle.

Grands Crus Bonnes-Mares (part), Clos du Tart, Clos de la Roche, Clos Saint Denis.

Premiers Crus Clos des Lambrays (or les Larrets), Clos Bussière, Monts-Luisants.

Chambolle-Musigny The favourite wines of many Burgundy lovers. They have an ideal balance of flavour and finesse. Their better Premiers Crus sell more expensively than many Grands Crus from other villages. As well as an outstanding red wine, le Musigny produces a minute crop of white wine.

Grands Crus le Musigny, Bonnes-Mares (part).
Premiers Crus Charmes, Amoureuses, les Combottes.

Growers Comte Georges de Vogüé, Clair-Däu, Prieur, Joseph Drouhin, Roumier, Dujac.

Vougeot The vineyards of this village are dominated by the Clos de Vougeot, the headquarters of the Chevaliers de Tastevin and the largest single vineyard on the Côte.

Grand Cru Clos Vougeot.
Premier Cru Clos Blanc de Vougeot (white wine), Clos de la Perrière.

Growers Héritier-Guyot, Pierre Ponnelle, Bertagna.

Vosne-Romanée This village is reputed to hold the most valuable agricultural land in France and the wines are justly renowned for their smooth richness.

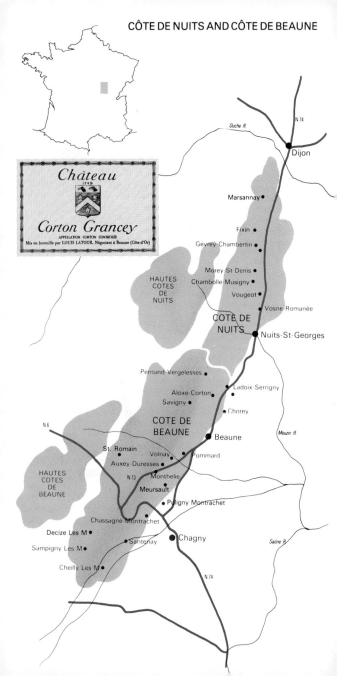

CÔTE DE NUITS AND CÔTE DE BEAUNE

Ouche R.

N.74

Dijon

Marsannay

Fixin

Gevrey-Chambertin

Morey-St-Denis

Chambolle-Musigny

HAUTES
COTES
DE
NUITS

Vougeot

Vosne-Romanée

CÔTE DE
NUITS

Nuits-St-Georges

Pernand-Vergelesses

Ladoix-Serrigny

Aloxe-Corton

Savigny

Chorey

CÔTE DE
BEAUNE

Beaune

Meuzin R.

N.6

St. Romain

Volnay

Pommard

Auxey-Duresses

Monthelie

HAUTES
COTES
DE
BEAUNE

N.73

Meursault

Puligny-Montrachet

Chassagne-Montrachet

Decize Les M

Chagny

Saône R.

Sampigny Les M

Santenay

Cheilly Les M

N.74

Château

1749

Corton Grancey

APPELLATION CORTON CONTROLÉE

Mis en bouteille par LOUIS LATOUR, Négociant à Beaune (Côte-d'Or)

Grands Crus Romanée-Conti, La Romanée, Romanée Saint-Vivant, La Tâche, Richebourg, Grands Echézeaux, Les Echézeaux.

Premiers Crus La Grand'Rue, Malconsorts, Suchots, Beaumonts.

Growers Domaine de la Romanée-Conti, Marey-Monge, Lamarche, Moillard, Latour, Clos Frantin, Charles Viénot, Noëllat.

Nuits-Saint-Georges Perhaps the Burgundian name best-known in Britain. As a result of supply having overtaken demand, prices have soared and many spurious wines have been passed off under this great name. The truth should be a full-bodied, deep-coloured wine, which matures rather earlier than the majority of the wines of the Côte de Nuits.

Premiers Crus les Saint-Georges, Murgers, Vaucrains, Porrets, Pruliers, Clos de la Maréchale, Clos d'Arlot, Clos des Forêts, Didiers.

Growers Hospice de Nuits, Faiveley, Moillard, Gouges.

Côte de Nuits Villages This appellation is for wine from one of a number of the lesser villages of the Côte de Nuits which do not have their own individual appellation. Of particular note is the single vineyard of Clos des Langres at Corgoloin.

Bourgogne Hautes Côtes de Nuits Until recently this wine was rarely seen, but the Nuits Saint-Georges company of Geisweiler has planted a large vineyard at Bévy and the wines are now coming on the market. They generally represent good value for money. Other growers include Jacob at Echevronne and Thévenot-le-Brun. The Cave Co-opérative des Hautes Côtes distributes much of the wine.

CÔTE DE BEAUNE

Ladoix-Serrigny Generally blended and sold as Côte de Beaune Villages, though several vineyards with the right to the Aloxe-Corton appellations lie within its boundaries.

Aloxe-Corton Its Grand Cru wine, Corton, is my favourite red wine from Burgundy, as I feel that it achieves the ideal balance between body, fruit and softness. The great white wine of Corton-Charlemagne also has many admirers.

Grands Crus Corton, Corton-Charlemagne, Charlemagne (this last has not been used for many years).

Premiers Crus Maréchaudes, Lolières.

Growers Louis Latour, Tollot-Beaut, Prince de Mérode, Jadot, Sénard, Dubreuil-Fontaine, Chandon de Briailles, Hospices de Beaune.

Pernand-Vergelesses Standing back in a narrow valley, this village is often overlooked though it produces much fine wine, both red and white.

Grands Crus Corton (part), Corton-Charlemagne (part).
Premiers Crus Ile de Vergelesses, les Basses Vergelesses.

Growers Chanson Père et Fils, Louis Latour, Chandon de Briailles, Dubreuil-Fontaine.

Chorey les Beaune Generally sold as Côte de Beaune Villages.
Growers Germain, Voarick.
Savigny Full-bodied, flavoursome red wines.

Premiers Crus Vergelesses, Dominode, Marconnets, Lavières, Redrescul, Narbantons.

Growers Bouchard Père et Fils, Chanson Père et Fils, Doudet-Naudin, Hospices de Beaune.

Beaune The largest vineyard town of the Côte de Beaune and the centre of the Burgundian wine trade. As the vineyards lie on two separate hills, the exposition, and the subsequent style of the wines, vary considerably. A little white wine is made, of which perhaps the best-known is the Clos des Mouches of Drouhin. In Beaune, many of the vineyards are in vertical strips up the hillside and the quality can vary considerably within a single vineyard; this is particularly true in the Grèves, where certain growers, notably Bouchard Père et Fils with their Vigne de l'Enfant Jésus, rate the wine amongst their very best, whilst others with vines at the bottom of the hill may rate their wines less highly.

Premiers Crus Fèves, Grèves, Bressandes, Clos du Roi, Marconnets, Teurons, Clos des Mouches, Champs-Pimont, Clos de la Mousse.

Growers Bouchard Père et Fils, Chanson Père et Fils, Hospices de Beaune, Darviot, Remoissenet, Louis Jadot, Albert Morot.

Volnay Rich wines, with a great deal of finesse. Considered by many to be the most attractive wines of Burgundy.

Premier Crus Caillerets, Champans, Chevret, Frémiets, Santenots, Clos des Chênes, Taille-Pieds.
Growers Marquis d'Angerville, Hospices de Beaune, Delagrange. Domaine de la Pousse d'Or, Henri Boillot, de Montille.

Pommard What Nuits-Saint-Georges is to the Englishman, Pommard is to the American; its very name seems to hold a fascination for him and as a result he has to pay more for the wine than its intrinsic merits often deserve. The wines are more full-bodied than most from the Côte de Beaune.

Premiers Crus Rugiens, Epenots, Arvelets, Clos de la Commaraine.

Growers Hospices de Beaune, Jaboulet-Vercherre, Parent, Comte Armand, Laplanche.

Monthelie One of the less well-known villages, whose wines often represent good value for money. Similar in style to a Volnay.

Premier Cru Champs-Fulliot.   **Growers** Ropiteau-Mignon, André Ropiteau, de Suremain.

Saint-Romain Rarely seen. I prefer the white to the red wines.

Grower Roland Thévenin.

Auxey-Duresses The red wines normally lack the distinction of the better wines of the Côte de Beaune; the white are similar to the lesser wines of Meursault.

Premier Crus les Duresses, Clos du Val.   **Growers** Roland Thévenin, Roy.

Meursault The centre of the white wine vineyards of the Côte d'Or and the scene of one of the three great banquets of the Hospices de Beaune Sale weekend, la Paulée de Meursault. A little red wine is made, but the village's reputation is firmly based on the full-bodied, nutty white wines – perhaps my favourites of all Burgundy.

Premiers Crus Genevrières, Charmes, Perrières, Gouttes d'Or, Poruzots.   **Growers** Ropiteau-Mignon, de Moucheron, Poupon, Prieur.

Blagny This name, which appears mainly on red wines, is that of a little primitive hamlet up on the hillside between Meursault and Puligny-Montrachet. Fine wine is made here, generally sold as Meursault.

Premiers Crus Pièce sous le Bois, Sous le Dos d'Ane.

Puligny-Montrachet The finest dry white wine producing village in the world, with a succession of great wines of the utmost distinction. The production is very tightly controlled, so prices are high.

Grands Crus le Montrachet (part), Chevalier Montrachet, Bâtard-Montrachet (part), Bienvenues-Bâtard-Montrachet.   **Growers** Leflaive, Comte Lafond, Roland Thévenin, Etienne Sauzet, Bouchard Père et Fils, Baron Thénard, Marquis de Laguiche.

Premiers Crus Cailleret, Combettes, Pucelles, Folatières, la Garenne.

Chassagne-Montrachet Though it perhaps has a wider reputation for its white wines (it has one Grand Cru and part of two others), it produces rather more red.

Grands Crus le Montrachet (part), Bâtard-Montrachet (part), Criots Bâtard Montrachet.   **Growers** Duc de Magenta, Delagrange-Bachelet, Ramonet, de Marcilly.

Premiers Crus Clos Saint Jean, Morgeot, Abbaye de Morgeot, la Maltroye, Cailleret.

Saint-Aubin A little seen appellation producing some interesting red wines and rather less white wine. Very rarely seen with a vineyard name.

Grower Raoul Clerget.

Santenay A very important village for red wines. There is a wide variety of styles of wine within the vineyards, as the geological structure of the soil is complicated; the slope, too, faces more south-east than the rest of the Côte d'Or. Some wines have the fullness of those of the Côte de Nuits, whilst others are much lighter and more delicate.

Premiers Crus Gravières, Clos des Tavannes, Passe Temps, Maladière.

Growers Domaine Saint Michel, G. Prieur, Mestre.

Dezize-les-Maranges, Cheilly-les-Maranges, Sampigny-les-Maranges are the three poor relations of the Côte d'Or. Indeed, they are not even in the Côte d'Or *département,* but in the Saône et Loire. For long they have sought the right to sell their wines under the name of Santenay, but this approach has always been rebuffed. Now they are invariably blended and sold as Côte de Beaune Villages.

Côte de Beaune A very small appellation consisting of almost 9 hectares of vineyards. Rarely seen.

Côte de Beaune Villages This wine can come from one or more of all the villages of the Côte de Beaune, except Aloxe-Corton, Beaune, Pommard, and Volnay. Often the coarseness of the wines of one village is balanced with the softness of those of another. As there is a lot of wine available, it should be of sound, consistent quality. Only red wines can be sold under this appellation.

Bourgogne Hautes-Côtes de Beaune A rather larger area than its sister appellation of the Côte de Nuits. As the climate is much cooler, the vintage is normally about ten days later than on the main Côte and this can cause problems in difficult years. Again, a great deal of the wine is made by the co-operative cellar, but others to look out for include the Château de Mandelot of Bouchard Père et Fils and those of such growers as Mazilly Père et Fils, Guillemard-Dupont and Joliot. One other wine worth mentioning is the rosé wine from the village of Orches, made from the Gamay grape and called Bourgogne Grand Ordinaire.

REGION DE MERCUREY

This is a small but increasingly important area, where a lot of replanting of vines is now gradually being done. Whilst much of the wine that is produced is under the generic Burgundian appellations, there are also four village names.

Mercurey The most reputed of the villages. The production under this name is large (more than that of any village of the Côte d'Or), as three other hamlets also share the appellation. The red wines are justly highly thought of and sell at much the same price as those of a village like Santenay. The production of white wine is much less important.

Premiers Crus Clos du Roi, Clos Voyen, Clos-Marcilly. (Other wines which can be recommended include Clos des Myglands and Clos la Marche.)

Growers Faiveley, Antonin Rodet, Bouchard Aîné, Protheau, Marcel Bureaux.

Rully A centre of sparkling wine production, as well as the making of crisp, white wines and full, soft red wines. Here, particularly, there has been considerable replanting of vineyards that had been allowed to revert to scrub.

Premiers Crus Mont-Palais, Meix-Caillet, Champ-Clou, la Renarde, Raclot.

Growers Jean-François Delorme, Domaine de la Folie, Monassier.

Givry Mainly known for its light red wines with a great deal of finesse. There are no Premier Cru vineyards, but the following vineyards are highly reputed: Cellier aux Moines, Clos Saint Paul, Clos Saint Pierre, Clos Salomon. The Beaune shipper, Remoissenet Père et Fils, makes a speciality of the wines of Givry, particularly Baron Thenard.

Montagny This appellation is only for white wines and has the distinction of having nothing but Premier Cru vineyards, though their names very rarely appear on the label. The Co-operative Cellar of Buxy produces much of the wine and that sold under the Louis Latour label is always worth buying.

MACONNAIS

The reputation of the area of Mâconnais for its wine rested firmly on its red wines made mainly from the Gamay. Over the past twenty years, though, the red vines have been uprooted and the Chardonnay has been planted. The white wines of Mâcon now probably represent the best value in Burgundy. Those from the better areas can be sold under the name Mâcon Villages and occasionally the village name itself will appear, as in Mâcon-Lugny or Mâcon-Viré.

The production is dominated by a number of co-operative cellars and the wine is distributed by the shippers of both Mâcon and Beaune. Single vineyard names are rare.

Towards the south of the area, just outside the town of Mâcon itself, lie the quality appellations of Saint-Véran, Pouilly-Loché, and Pouilly-Vinzelles. Their reputation is overshadowed by the great wine of the region:

Pouilly-Fuissé These vineyards lie in a natural amphitheatre, which catches the full force of the sun. Here the heaviest white wines of Burgundy are produced. Their full richness and comparatively low acidity have won them numerous admirers. Indeed, demand has often outstripped supply, with a sad effect on the price. Single vineyard names are again rare but the Château de Fuissé and the Château de Pouilly both make excellent wines.

BEAUJOLAIS

If the production of Burgundy were to be considered as a pyramid, then Beaujolais would be its base, for it is from here that the vast mass of the wine comes. Nearly all of it is red, made from the Gamay grape, though there is a little white, made from the Chardonnay (notably the Château de Loyse and the Château de Chatelard).

In the south of the region, to the north of Lyons and south of Villefranche, is the Bas-Beaujolais, dominated by a number of co-operative cellars producing easy-quaffing wines, a large proportion of which is sold as Beaujolais Nouveau just a month or so after the vintage. Quantities are sold by the glass in the bars of Paris and Lyons.

To the north lie thirty-six villages, whose wines can be sold as Beaujolais Villages. These wines have more body and fruit than Beaujolais Nouveau and are probably best drunk one to two years old. As in the Mâcon Villages, sometimes a village name appears, such as Beaujolais-Vaux, from the village of Vaux which claims to be the inspiration for Clochemerle.

The aristocracy of the Beaujolais is nine single names; each represents a particular style of wine.

Brouilly The largest of the Crus, soft, light wines which should be drunk before they are three years old. The Château de la Chaize is to be recommended.

Côte de Brouilly This wine comes from the slopes of Mont Brouilly and tends to be rather stronger than other Beaujolais. It can be drunk up to five years old in a good vintage. Look out for Château Thivin.

Chiroubles Full-bodied wines with a lot of fruit.

Fleurie The name evokes the style of the wines, for they are very flowery and elegant, showing at their best at about four years old. The co-operative cellar makes excellent wines and Aux Quatre Vents is one of the best vineyards.

Moulin à Vent From here come the greatest wines of the Beaujolais, deep in colour and full of flavour. They are capable of lasting ten years or more in the best years and sell as expensively as many Côte d'Or wines. The best vineyards include Château Portier and les Carquelins.

Chénas These wines are similar to those of Moulin à Vent, but lack the intensity of flavour. Château Bonnet produces some of the best.

Juliénas After Fleurie, perhaps my favourite wines in the Beaujolais. At their best, they are very elegant, with the rich fruit of the Gamay grape. They are best drunk two to three years old. The co-operative cellar can be relied on for good wines and others worth seeking out include the Château de Juliénas, les Capitans and those from the Domaine de Beauvernais.

Saint-Amour Early maturing, easy-drinking wines without great pretensions. Les Thevenins is my favourite growth.

Vintages

1980
The latest vintage for about forty years. Mixed quality, so much care is needed.

1979
Very varied reds, rather better than expected. The whites are more reliable.

1978
Excellent Beaujolais and very good wines from elsewhere in Burgundy.

1977
Generally speaking, thin and wishy-washy wines. Beaujolais Nouveau was a disaster and there is little of great interest to be found.

1976
A great vintage throughout Burgundy, with the possible exception of Chablis, where it was no more than very good.

1975
Chablis made the best wines; for the growers there it was a great year. Elsewhere the white wines were generally good and the red wines were disappointing.

1974
Not one of my favourite vintages. The reds are deep-coloured and mature. The whites are average, with a small production in the best villages of the Côte de Beaune.

1973
An enormous crop; the red wines from the Côte d'Or are at their peak, if they have not passed it. They have turned out better than a lot of people, myself included, expected. The white wines included some notable successes.

1972
Excellent value for money in the red wines. They had enormous initial acidity, but are now showing very well and will last. Worth seeking out. The whites have always been ugly.

1971
Very little wine was made, but it is of outstanding quality. A great vintage.

1970
A commercial vintage. You would be lucky to find anything which has not passed its best.

Earlier vintages to look out for, for red wines particularly: 1969, 1966, 1961, 1959, 1957, 1955, 1953, 1949, 1947, 1945, 1937, 1929, 1923.

ALSACE
Whether the river Rhine or the Vosges Mountains should provide the natural frontier between France and Germany has been the cause of fighting between the two countries for centuries. In the middle have been the vineyards of Alsace. The result is a tradition of viticulture and wines that owes much to both countries, but which is typical of neither.

The vineyards stretch in a narrow band along the foothills of the Vosges for about 80 kilometres, from Thann, north-west of Mulhouse, to Marlenheim, west of Strasbourg, with a further small enclave of vines on the German frontier, around Wissembourg, 60 kilometres to the north. The vineyards face generally east and benefit from the driest climate in France north of Perpignan. The nature of the soil varies widely from granitic schist to chalk. Partly because of this, there is a range of grape varieties, each one growing best on a particular type of soil.

It is an area of smallholdings, with approximately 9,500 families cultivating about 12,000 hectares of vines in 120 different villages. Of this number of growers only a third own more than a hectare of vines. The average annual production is about 115 million bottles. All wine has to be bottled in the area of production (the two *départements* of the Haut- and the Bas-Rhin) into Alsatian 'flute' bottles.

Because of the vast number of small growers, co-operative cellars are important, accounting for more than a quarter of the total wine produced; about a quarter of the production is sold by the growers direct; and the rest passes through the hands of the merchants or *négociants*.

Classification of wines
The vast majority of the wines of Alsace are sold under the name of a grape variety, and this means each wine is made 100 per cent from this grape. Occasionally, the grape name is joined to that of a village (for example, Riesling d'Ammerschwihr). A new classification, Grand Cru, is slowly coming into effect. It is envisaged that something over ninety of the best vineyards in Alsace will be allowed to have their names on the label, together with specific grape varieties, which might vary, depending on the soils concerned. Amongst the better known vineyards are: Rangen from Thann, Kitterlé (Guebwiller), Zinnkoepfle (Soultzmatt), Eichberg (Eguisheim), Hengst (Wintzenheim), Eichberg, Brand (Turckheim), Kaefferkopf (Ammerschwihr), Schlossberg (Kientzheim), Mamburg (Sigolsheim), Mandelberg (Mitterwihr), Sonnenglanz (Beblenheim), Sporen, Schoenenburg (Riquewihr), Kirchberg and Zahnacker (Ribeauville) from the Haut-Rhin, and Zotzenberg (Mittelbergheim),

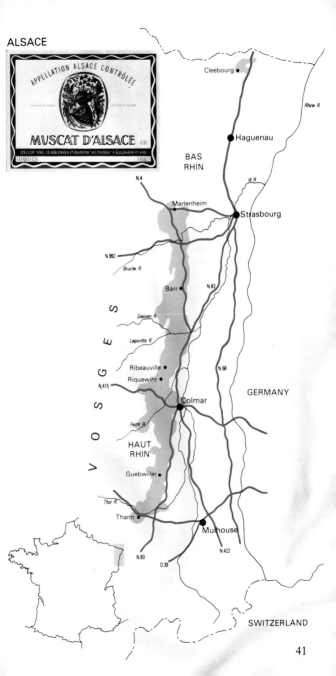

ALSACE

APPELLATION ALSACE CONTRÔLÉE

MUSCAT D'ALSACE

Cleebourg

Rhine R.

Haguenau

BAS
RHIN

Ill. R.

N.4

Marlenheim

Strasbourg

N.992

Bruche R.

Barr

N.83

Giessen R.

Leepvritte R.

Ribeauville

Riquewihr

N.415

Colmar

GERMANY

Fecht R.

HAUT
RHIN

Guebwiller

Thor. R.

Thann

Mulhouse

N.83

D.39

N.422

SWITZERLAND

V O S G E S

N.68

41

Freiberg, Gaensbrunnel, Zisser (Barr), Clos Sainte Odile (Obernai) from the Bas-Rhin.

Any wine that is made from a blend of grapes or from one of the lesser reputed varieties is sold either under a brand name, or under the name Edelzwicker.

All Alsatian wines are fermented out and are basically dry. Richer wines are made by latepicking, when the label may say Vendange Tardive, the equivalent of the German Spät-lese. In certain rare cases in an exceptional year, individual super-ripe grapes may be picked, giving a wine called Selection de Grains Nobles (Beerenauslese).

In order to distinguish between varying qualities of wines, some shippers use such terms as Cuvée Tradition, Réserve Exceptionelle and Sélection Personelle. These have no legal significance and are personal to the shipper or grower concerned.

So that they may gain extra recognition, wines are frequently entered for the various wine fairs. The most commonly seen medals on Alsatian wines come from Colmar, the national wine fair at Mâcon and the Concours Agricole at Paris. Of more distinction is a wine that bears the seal of the Confrèrie Saint Etienne, which means that it has been submitted to one of their tasting panels and has been recognized as being outstanding of its type.

Grape varieties

RIESLING The greatest of Alsatian grape varieties, accounting for about 13 per cent of the area under vines. It is late to ripen and gives a very clean, full-bodied, crisp wine, which makes the ideal accompaniment for *choucroute* (the aristocratic cousin of the German sauerkraut), salmon or even shellfish.

GEWÜRZTRAMINER The speciality wine of Alsace; this grape variety produces no other wine to equal it elsewhere in the world. It is full of flavour, with a spiciness all of its own. A very easy wine for the wine-beginner to enjoy.

MUSCAT Again, a very fruity wine, which has the full flavour of the Muscat grape, but is completely dry. Its overpowering taste causes some problems when one tries to match it with a food. Because of this, the Alsatians suggest that it should be drunk by itself as an aperitif.

PINOT GRIS or TOKAY D'ALSACE A very full-bodied wine, high in alcohol. It lacks the flavour of the three previous wines, but is an ideal accompaniment for foie gras.

PINOT NOIR The great grape of Burgundy produces fresh, light, fruity featherweights in Alsace. These are made to satisfy the demand from tourists for a red wine, though in nearly all cases it is much more like a rosé. Because of this demand the plantings in this variety are increasing faster than those for any other.

The above five are the great varieties of Alsace. Close behind them come:

SYLVANER The speciality of the Bas-Rhin, where, in certain vineyards, it can produce exceptional wines. Elsewhere, for the most part, it makes a fresh carafe wine. It is the most widely planted variety in Alsace.

CLEVNER or KLEVNER The Pinot, in its numerous sub-varieties appears under this name. It is probably at its best in the extreme north at Cleebourg. Generally, it is a crisp neutral wine, rather low in acidity. It is often used for making sparkling wine.

Certain other varieties are planted, but their name must not appear on the label. The most important of these is the Chasselas, which is mostly found in the Haut-Rhin. Others include the Muller-Thurgau, the Knipperlé and the Goldriesling, but they are of insignificant and lessening importance. The Klevner de Heiligenstein is a sub-variety of the Gewürztraminer, but may appear under its own name in a very restricted area of the Bas-Rhin. The total area is less than 5 hectares.

Co-operatives Eguisheim, Westhalten, Beblenheim, Ribeauville, Cleebourg.

Growers Zind-Humbrecht, Schlumberger, SickDreyer.

Vintages
1980
Almost no Gewürztraminer produced, otherwise a small vintage of light drinkable wines.
1979
A good yield of fair, but not really great wines.
1978
A very good year as far as the quality is concerned, but almost no Muscat and very little Gewürztraminer was produced.
1977
Rather ordinary wines, without staying power.

1976
Excellent, full-bodied wines, which will keep well. Some very good Vendange Tardive wines made.
1975
Good wines, though perhaps short on body.
1973
Very good wines, which should be drunk now.
1971
Great wines, of which the Rieslings and the Gewürztraminers particularly are still showing well.

Vesle R.

Ardre R.

Reims

Gueux

Pargny

Villedommange • 0.26

Villers

Rilly

MONTAGNE D

D.71

Vandières

Hautvillers • Champillon

Chatillon sur Marne

Venteuil

Damery

Cumières

Avenay

Marne R.

Dormans

VALLÉE DE LA MARNE

Ay

Epernay

Mareuil sur Av

Oir

Pierry

Choully

D.9

Vinay

Cramant

Monthelon

Grauves •

Avize

Oger

Le Mesnil sur Oger

CÔTE DES

N 3

N 33

Vertus

Bergère les Vertus

Étoges

N 51

CHAMPAGNE

'Le Champagne' is the wine and 'La Champagne' the region
which is the most northern vineyard of France, comprising
the *départements* of the Ardennes, Marne, Haute-Marne and
Aube. The area devoted to wine is today not so great as it
was, but 34,000 hectares are in the defined region, of which
24,200 are actually under vines. The climate is not particularly cold, but it can be damp and production varies in quantity
as well as quality: for example, in 1978 594,732 hectolitres of
wine were made, and in 1979, 1,731,598 hectolitres.

The word 'Champagne' means 'open countryside' and the
landscape is undulating. The friable topsoil in the main wine

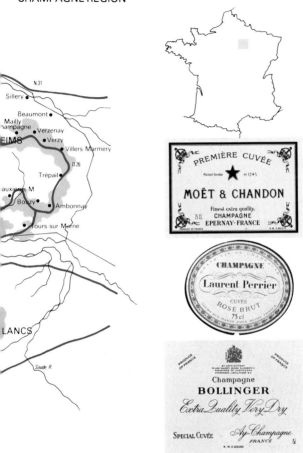

areas is a shallow layer over a huge blanket of chalk, containing fossils – excellent for producing elegant, vivacious white wines. Indeed, this layer of chalk goes under the English Channel to emerge as the white cliffs of Dover.

Types of Champagne

Although some of the big Champagne establishments own vineyards, none could operate only with the grapes of their own properties; thousands of proprietors, some of them owning what are true smallholdings, make up the Champagne vineyard. Some of these run plots owned by others, some make their own wine and then sell it to one of the big establishments, some market their grapes to be processed by the Champagne houses. It is important to realize that every stage of Champagne production, in addition to the grapes and their cultivation, is strictly controlled: for example, the wine cannot be made anywhere outside the defined region even if the grapes have been grown within it, buying grapes can only be done with a permit from the Comité Inter-professional du Vin de Champagne (the CIVC). The tiny code letters and numbers on the label of every bottle of the wine enable identification of who made it to be swift and everything that goes on that label is subject to controls as well.

The bulk of Champagne is non-vintage. The variations in the climate mean that the high acidity of one year can balance the softness and marked fruit of another. Most houses make several styles of wine, however, and 'B.O.B.' or 'Buyer's Own Brand' is a Champagne specially prepared for a certain customer; as such wines do not have to bear the high costs of advertising, they can be sold at slightly lower prices without this in any way reflecting on their quality – they may have come from a famous establishment.

VINTAGE CHAMPAGNE is the wine of a single year, and varies according to the style of that year. But it is permitted to add up to 20 per cent of the wine from another vintage if this will benefit and balance the wine. Vintage Champagne is considered to be at its best when it is between seven and twelve years from the date on the label, but this naturally varies and some people, including myself, like fine old wines even if they have lost a little of their vigour.

PINK CHAMPAGNE is made either by allowing the skins of black grapes to remain in the must long enough to tint it, or by blending a little of the red wine of certain Champagne villages. Bouzy is, for obvious reasons, a famous village name, but there are several others.

BLANC DE BLANCS is made from white grapes only and sometimes may even be labelled as 'Blanc de Chardonnay'. It is elegant, delicate and crisp, but it is quite wrong to suppose that it is 'the best'.

BLANC DE NOIRS is made from black grapes only. This is a rarity outside the region, but the wines of Aÿ are especially fine in this category – as, indeed, they are in general.

CREMANT wines have a little less fizz than ordinary Champagnes – between 3·5 and 4·5 atmospheres – whereas a fully *mousseux* sparkling wine has about 5·6 atmospheres, or pressure behind the cork. They can be equally delicious.

SINGLE VINEYARD WINES are unusual but interesting – worth sampling if you visit the region.

DE LUXE CHAMPAGNES are the wines that each establishment considers its very finest. They may be vintage, non-vintage, blanc de blancs or not; some come from specially fine vineyard sites. Dom Pérignon is the most famous, but there are many others, including Dom Ruinart; Belle Epoque and Blason de France of Perrier-Jouët; Cristal Brut of Louis Roederer; Cuvée William Deutz of Deutz and Geldermann; Cuvée Diamant Bleu of Heidsieck Dry Monopole. They are expensive and highly individual. At least two houses, Krug and Pol Roger, do not make a luxury wine because they feel that their non-vintage and vintage wines are the very best anyway. Bollinger makes 'RD', to signify 'recently disgorged', meaning that the wine has had extra maturation on its first cork.

COTEAUX CHAMPENOIS is the term now given to the still wines of the Champagne region which are mostly white, although some red is made.

Bottles come in a wide range of sizes but generally the quarter-bottles and those bigger than magnum (two-bottle) size will have been transferred under pressure, because the big bottles are too awkward to shake, and the little ones too small. The magnum is considered almost the perfect size as there is less air in proportion to the wine, which results in first-rate maturation.

Dosage is the term used to indicate how much additional sweetening has been added to the wine: *brut* is very dry; *extra-dry* or *extra-sec* is fairly dry; *sec* will seem slightly sweet; *demi-sec* is definitely sweet; *doux* or *rich* is sweet. The fine sweet

Champagnes are superb between-times drinks or to partner sweet dishes, so they should not be neglected if they can be found. Most people like a dry wine as an aperitif, a little fuller style with food.

Grape varieties

PINOT NOIR is the main black grape, contributing fruit and body to the wines.

CHARDONNAY is the main white grape, contributing elegance and finesse.

PINOT MEUNIER is also grown, and two other varieties are permitted by law, but it is the Pinot Noir and the Chardonnay that are the most important varieties.

The Champagne process

Champagne can never be cheap, because of the high – and ever-increasing – price of grapes and the detailed skill and time it takes to make the wine. It is wholly a quality product. The method by which it is made is complex and is used to produce the finest sparkling wines of the world, although in the EEC and Spain only those actually produced in the defined Champagne region can be called 'Champagne'; other wine labels may proudly indicate that the wine is made by the same method. There is, indeed, no sparkling wine that is really like Champagne, however good it may be.

First the grapes are crushed and then the 'must' is allowed to ferment and be changed by the action of yeasts into wine, just as with still wines. Normally, both black and white grapes are used. As the winter weather causes the temperature to drop, the yeasts stop working and the wine lies quiet; in the early spring, before the warm weather makes them start working again, the chief winemakers in the Champagne houses compose the *cuvée* or vatting, blending the wines from different vineyards and different grapes to make a harmonious wine in accordance with their 'house style' and any special wines they wish to produce. Then the wine is bottled before its fermentation starts again, so that the carbon dioxide that would otherwise escape from the fermentation vat is imprisoned in the wine, and remains there as the seedpearl-like bubbles.

The wine is corked, either with a cork held down by a metal clip or, more often nowadays, with a crown cork. It can remain on this 'first cork' for many years, in the miles of galleries cut out of the chalk below Reims and Epernay (the curious, flask-shaped *crayères* at Reims were excavated by the Romans). At least one establishment has 25 kilometres of these galleries, holding the millions of bottles essential for the reserve stock that must never run too low.

As the wine cannot be filtered before bottling, it is not 'star bright' and particles will remain in it. So for about three months the bottles are put neck down in wooden frames called *pupitres,* where highly skilled workers come round to shake and turn them every day; this process, which is called *remuage,* involves both shaking the bottle from side to side and slinging the wine around vigorously – it sounds like giants playing castanets! Eventually, as each bottle is given a slight final turn and inclined more steeply, the deposit slides down on to the first cork, to which it sticks. The bottles are binned upside down, the corks of one row resting in the punts of those below. Like this, they can remain in their home cellars for many years.

Before the bottles are sold this deposit must be removed. The neck of the bottle is put into a freezing solution, the first cork is unclipped, taking the deposit with it in a pellet of ice. The bottle is topped up with a little cane sugar dissolved in wine (the dosage), according to the degree of ultimate sweetness required, and the second cork (which is composed of layers of cork) goes in, and is fastened with a wire muzzle. The bottle is 'dressed' with the long foil capsule, labelled and then given a little more maturation before being despatched to its purchaser. After the insertion of the second cork, the wine ages more rapidly.

The wines

Some well-known Champagne brands are as follows:

Ayala Light, gracious, invariably well-bred, the vintage wines especially good.

Bollinger Noble, impressive, possibly a little austere for some, but a great wine for the appreciative.

Canard Duchène Pleasing, with a touch of 'allure', rounded and fullish.

Castellane Brisk and elegant, lightish in body, crisp.

George Goulet A smooth, engaging wine, polished and trim – their *cremant* is outstanding.

Alfred Gratien Trim and zippy, with sufficient weight to serve with food although it is good by itself.

Heidsieck Dry Monopole An assertive, almost scented wine, definitely well-bred.

Charles Heidsieck A big, mouth-filling wine but very definitely assertive because of its dryness.

Piper-Heidsieck A full, dry wine in general, for those who like a zippy Champagne with some assertiveness.

Henriot Flowery and gracious, a little light but with charm.

Louis Kremer Elegant and close-knit, good for those who like a crisp wine – it might be too much so for some.

Krug Always a majestic full wine, though recently they made their Grande Cuvée non-vintage lighter in style. Definitely can be drunk with food and always impressive.

Lanson Fullish in style, crisp and perky – slightly assertive.

Mailly Full and firm, not aggressively dry, definitely of interest as it comes from the named area only.

Marguerite Christel 'Pretty' in every sense, well-made, charming, good for aperitifs or end of meal sweet dishes.

Mercier Good, slightly soft but weighty enough to stand up to party atmospheres as well as party food.

Moët et Chandon Full fragrance, some weight and slight softness which makes it good for many occasions.

G.H. Mumm Obviously fragrant, moderately full in flavour and well-made – a biggish, classy wine.

Joseph Perrier Well-balanced and the slight softness does not detract from its fruity, appealing style.

Laurent Perrier Straightforward and easy to enjoy, trimly made and useful for many purposes.

Perrier-Jouet A somewhat fruity, appealing wine, with a definite chic because it is so well made.

Pol Roger Charming, delicate, a craftsman's Champagne with excellent balance – not for those who like the obvious.

Pommery A beautiful wine consistently, with ripe, enticing bouquet and delicate but definite flavour.

Louis Roederer Invariably noble, with a splendid bouquet, subtle flavours and admirable balance.

St Marceaux Taut, trim and also very well made, with many subtleties of flavour – not, perhaps, for anyone who does not like dry wines with a nervous intensity.

Saint Simon Good, well-made – excellent for parties.

Salon A rare and fine wine, closely-knit with finesse.

Taittinger Light, elegant, with much finesse, perhaps too delicately aristocratic for a mixed party.

De Venoge This establishment is the great specialist in BOB but the wine under their own label is excellently made.

Veuve Clicquot Ponsardin A big but well-bred wine, ripe with an assertive bouquet and full flavour.

Vintages

It is not really possible to list vintage years for Champagne. This is because it is up to the individual Champagne establishment to decide whether or not they will make a vintage wine in any one year. Some houses make very little vintage wine, others only select certain *cuvées* for the purpose.

The situation becomes even more complicated when one considers that, even if an establishment does make a vintage Champagne, it may decide to release this to the French market only, or to reserve the whole lot for export. Tastes of different markets vary, and distribution of vintage Champagne is therefore uneven.

Serving Champagne

As this wine is inevitably expensive, it is worth taking trouble to serve it correctly. The goblet, tulip or straight-sided glass is suitable, the shallow saucer is not because it flattens the wine. Glasses must be absolutely clean, dried with cloths untainted by detergent which flatten the wine and cause it to acquire a horrible smell. Temperature should be cool, but not semi-frozen; allow an hour in the fridge or fifteen minutes in a deep bucket of ice and water. When opening a bottle, always have a cloth around it to protect your hand, and never point it at anyone: annually, many people lose an eye because they will not take care. If a cork seems stiff, prise it gently upwards or run the hot tap over the neck of the bottle for a few seconds, when increased pressure will push the cork out. Always twist the bottle – not the cork; if you twist the cork, you are likely to break off the top of the 'mushroom' and will then have to pierce the remainder with a needle in order to release the gas before using a corkscrew to remove the cork.

THE RHÔNE VALLEY

Two great rivers start from the same Swiss glacier, the Rhine flowing north and the Rhône south. In the Rhône Valley, between Vienne and Avignon, the vineyards are grouped in two distinct areas separated by an 80-kilometre stretch of fertile agricultural land. The vineyards in the northern sector are mainly on the hillsides east and west of the river where they are subjected to the very strong force of the Mistral wind, which blows hot in the summer and cold in the winter. The vines are pruned, and sometimes tied together in threes, to be able to withstand this fierce wind. There are many variations of soil in the area, ranging from brownish clay to light chalk.

NORTHERN RHÔNE VALLEY

1. Côtes-du-Rhône
3. Côte Rôtie
4. Condrieu
5. Château-Grillet
6. Hermitage
7. Crozes Hermitage
8. St-Joseph
9. Cornas
10. St-Péray
17. Clairette de die

SOUTHERN RHÔNE VALLEY

1. Côtes-du-Rhône
2. Côtes-du-Rhône Villages
11. Châteauneuf-du-Pape
12. Lirac
13. Tavel
14. Beaumes de Venise
15. Gigondas
16. Rasteau
18. Coteaux du Tricastin
19. Côtes du Ventoux
20. Côtes du Luberon

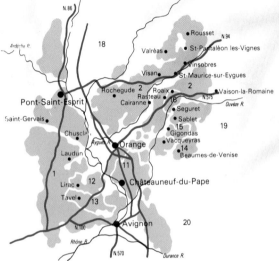

On the southern plain there are gently undulating hills, and
terraces of large stones characterize many of the vineyards.
No less than twenty-three varieties of vine are permitted to
be grown in the area and these combine with the different
soils to produce an infinite variation of fine red, white and
rosé wines.

About 40,000 hectares are under wine and there are over
9,000 registered vignerons. These range from proprietors of
smallholdings who normally sell their grapes to the local
co-operative to the larger estates where the proprietors make
and bottle their own wines, frequently exporting their finest
selections all over the world.

An average vintage will produce the equivalent of 250
million bottles, though only a small proportion is bottled in
the area of production.

Classification of wines

The major part of the Rhône crop is sold under the name of Côtes-du-Rhône. The second largest class of wines is from sixteen selected parishes which are allowed to sell their produce as Côtes-du-Rhône Villages. These wines are better than basic Côtes-du-Rhône. The very best areas in the Rhône Valley are known by the thirteen different appellations under which their production is controlled.

From north to south, the appellations are: Côte Rôtie, Condrieu, Château Grillet, Crozes-Hermitage, Hermitage, St-Joseph, Cornas, St-Péray, Tricastin, Gigondas, Châteauneuf-du-Pape, Lirac, and Tavel.

Most Rhône white wines are dry and grapey and the red wines, thanks to abundant sunshine, are full-bodied and rich in flavour. The lighter, more fruity reds are best drunk young. Rhône rosé wines are dry with an orange rather than a pink tinge. A very small quantity of sweet wine is made in the style of port (where fermentation of the sweet grape juice is stopped by the addition of alcohol). These wines are known as *vin doux naturel*. There is also some white dry full-bodied sparkling wine, which is made in St-Peray by the Champagne method.

Many excellent Rhône wines are exhibited at wine fairs in their areas of production and the very finest often achieve success at the French National Wine Fair at Mâcon or the Concours Agricole in Paris.

Grape varieties

The large variety of vines grown in the Rhône Valley enable the *vigneron* to produce exactly the style of wine he requires. The individual grapes have very strong personalities and are rarely offered on their own. Blending of red and white grapes is a vital part of Rhône wine production as the white grapes temper the fire and strength of the red.

GRENACHE This variety is the backbone for the very productive vineyards in the southern Rhône area and is ideally cultivated on slopes producing wines with body, good alcoholic strength and rugged firmness.

SYRAH The Syrah is one of the most important black grapes in the Rhône, giving body, vigour and colour to red wines. It produces very aromatic and long-lived wines which require cask and bottle maturing.

CLAIRETTE An excellent black grape vine which yields well in poor soils, producing light and elegant wines.

BOURBOULENC A vigorous black grape variety which makes light wines that are ideal for blending with heavier varieties.

CARIGNAN A vine well-adapted to poor soil, producing balanced wines with good keeping qualities that are frequently blended with Grenache (particularly for making rosé wines).

CINSAULT A black grape vine which produces well on stony soil. The wines are light, fruity and elegant.

VIOGNIER A rare white grape vine which produces superbly characteristic wines in Condrieu and Château Grillet. It is also grown in Côte Rôtie where it is used to temper the fire of the Syrah.

MARSANNE and ROUSANNE The two white varieties mainly used in the four appellations, Hermitage, Crozes-Hermitage, St-Joseph and St-Péray. They produce full-bodied wines which are fresh in their youth and which age magnificently into very full-bodied dry wines.

Many other varieties are planted and in Châteauneuf-du-Pape the law allows up to thirteen different types of grape to be used.

Growers Baron le Roy, Nicolet, Sabon, Vernay, Multier, Guigal, Vidal-Fleury, Jaboulet, Chapoutier, Chave, Meffre, Delas, Ogier.

Co-operatives Tain Hermitage, Tavel, Cairanne, Vaison-la-Romaine, Beaumes de Venise, Valréas (Enclave des Papes), Rasteau, and many others.

Vintages
1979
Good yield with very reasonable quality.
1978
High yield of very good wines.
1977
Average yield, very pleasant wines.
1976
Above average yield of good wines, the best of which are not yet ready.

1975
Low yield, wines for drinking now. The whites are better than the reds.
1973
Above average yield, a good red wine vintage.
1971
Low yield with some really excellent wines.

THE LOIRE VALLEY

The Loire, the longest river in France (960 kilometres), has its source in the mountains of the Massif Central in the Ardèche. Most of the Loire benefits from a microclimate. The forests to the north protect it from the cold winds of the plateau, while the vineyards facing south towards the Loire have the advantage of cool sea breezes with less rainfall. The summer days are bright and hot. The soil is mainly a mixture of pebbles and granitic sands, over limestone subsoil.

It is an area of smallholdings, ranging from less than 1 hectare to 40 hectares. There is a total of 60,000 hectares of vines, producing 1,340,000 hectolitres of wine, 550,000 hectolitres of which is red and rosé wine. Therefore, it is mainly a region for white wine.

Nowadays, the trend is for the growers to sell their wine directly, and there is a decreasing number of *négociants*. Large co-operative cellars are important throughout the Loire.

Classification of wines

The wines are named after the region of production, except for Muscadet which is sold under the name of the grape variety. Each regional group is further subdivided into the appellation applying to the region. In this case the type of grape is indicated on the label, meaning it is made 100 per cent from this grape. The vineyard name is sometimes shown on the label. When it is surrounded by a wall which protects the vines and therefore enhances the quality of the end product, it is called a *clos* (enclosure).

The wines
Sancerre, Pouilly Fumé, Quincy, and Reuilly

This region, on the eastern part of the Loire, is famous for its white wines produced from the Sauvignon grape, making a dry, fruity, slightly musky, and spicy wine which should be drunk young, and not aged more than six years. White wine called Pouilly sur Loire is made predominantly from the Chasselas grape. Some very good red wine is produced from the Pinot Noir grape, of Burgundy fame, at Sancerre, Menetou-Salon and Reuilly. It has a characteristic cherry nose. In good years, such as 1971, 1975 and 1976 these red wines should be matured at least five years in bottle.

Vouvray and Montlouis

In the Touraine region at the heart of the Loire are produced white wines made 100 per cent from the Chenin Blanc grape, locally known as the Pineau de la Loire. These wines may be dry, semi-sweet, or sweet, depending largely on the type of year. In sunny years like 1976, the wine tends to be sweeter.

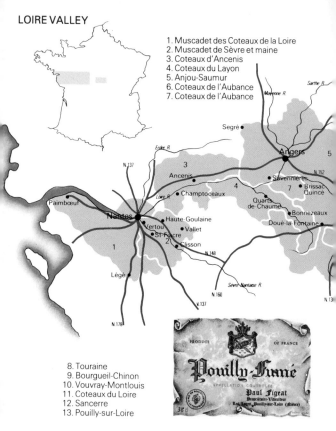

LOIRE VALLEY

1. Muscadet des Coteaux de la Loire
2. Muscadet de Sèvre et maine
3. Coteaux d'Ancenis
4. Coteaux du Layon
5. Anjou-Saumur
6. Coteaux de l'Aubance
7. Coteaux de l'Aubance

8. Touraine
9. Bourgueil-Chinon
10. Vouvray-Montlouis
11. Coteaux du Loire
12. Sancerre
13. Pouilly-sur-Loire

In this case the growers wait until the *pourriture noble* has set in, as in the Sauternes region of Bordeaux, before picking the grapes. The harvest is usually between 15 October and 15 November, so this is one of the last regions in France for grape picking. Both dry and sweet wine should be matured five years in bottle to develop its full fruit.

Chinon, Bourgueil and Saint Nicolas de Bourgueil
The famous red wines of Touraine, made from Cabernet Franc and sometimes blended with up to 15 per cent Cabernet Sauvignon grape. The wine is ruby in colour, often characterized by a perfume of violet, raspberry and blackberry which develops into a fully truffly, vanilla, or oaky scent as it ages. It should be matured in bottle for five years and in a good year like 1975 and 1976 it can age over twenty years. Some good dry rosé wine is also produced here.

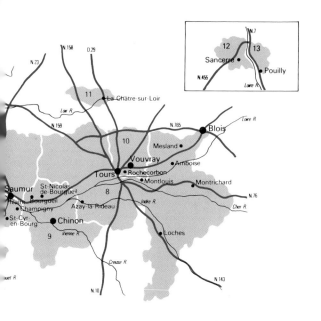

Touraine The Touraine vineyard is subdivided into the regions of Touraine, Touraine Amboise, Touraine Azay-le-Rideau, and Touraine Mesland. The red wines are made mainly from the Gamay grape, of Beaujolais fame. The white wines come from Sauvignon or Chenin Blanc grapes.

Anjou and Saumur This area produces white wine from the Chenin Blanc, which ranges from dry to sweet depending on the vintage, and is very similar in style to Vouvray. The most famous dry white wine comes from the Cru Savennières at La Coulée de Serrant, a mere 3 hectares owned by Madame Joly. The Sauternes-like sweet whites come from the Coteaux de Layon, the best ones from Bonnezeaux and Quarts de Chaume. Both dry and sweet wines should be matured for five years and the sweet ones can age over twenty years to produce rich, liqueur-like wines.

The red wines are made mainly from Cabernet Franc and Cabernet Sauvignon grapes. These can be called Cabernet d'Anjou but the most famous is the Saumur Champigny.

Some sweet rosé wine is also made from both Cabernet varieties, as well as some Pineau d'Aunis. Here, they come under the appellation Rosé d'Anjou, mainly from Brissac.

Muscadet, produced near Nantes, is a dry light white wine with a greenish tinge, made from the Muscadet grape originally known as Melon de Bourgogne. This grape is picked early, fermentation is slow, and the wine is often kept a long time on its sediment, unracked. This process, known as *sur lie,* ensures that the wine is supple and fruity, and keeps a slight prickle which can be felt on the tongue. It is an ideal accompaniment for shellfish. The main sector for Muscadet is Sèvre-et-Maine.

Sparkling wines Some sparkling, *méthode champenoise,* wine is made in Touraine at Vouvray and Montlouis, and in Anjou mainly at Saumur. The base wine from the Chenin Blanc grape should not exceed 11° alcohol. 20g of sugar is added to cause a second fermentation in bottle lasting two months and producing the carbonic gaz. The extent of effervescence is governed by the amount of sugar added to the wine. The less sparkling wines called *pétillant* have a gaz pressure of $2.5 kg/cm^2$, while the *mousseux* have a pressure of $4.5 kg/cm^2$. A surprising characteristic of these wines is that they can mature very well in bottle to produce a fuller, fruitier flavour.

The Cremant de Loire is another sparkling wine which gained its new appellation in 1975. Monsieur Latheron at Amboise is the prime innovator of this wine made from a blend of seven grape varieties; Chenin Blanc, Pinot Noir, Chardonnay, Cabernet Franc, Cabernet Sauvignon, Pineau d'Aunis and Menu Pineau. Unlike ordinary sparkling wines, the production of this one is governed by strict regulations, as for Champagne.

Vintages
1979
A fair yield of good red and dry white wines.
1978
A good year for quality red wines which can be aged, and dry white wines.
1977
Poor quantity of light, often chaptalized (when sugar is added to increase the alcohol level) red and dry white wines due to frost damage in late spring and lack of sunshine.

1976
Excellent quality red and semi-sweet to sweet white wines, which will keep very well.
1975
Very good quality red and sweet white wines which will mature.
1974
Harsh red, but very good dry white wines.
1972
Poor yield but well-developed red and dry white wines.

1971
Very good red and sweet white wines which can be aged.

1970
Very good red and exceptional dry white, wines ready for drinking.

Growers Huet, Darragon in Vouvray. Couly, Joguet, J.M. Raffault in Chinon. Darmé, Lamé Delille Boucard in Bourgueil. Douet in Doué La Fontaine, Saumur. Figeat in Pouilly Fumé. Sauvion in Muscadet. Pellé in Menetou Salon.

Négociants Marc Bredif in Vouvray, Audebert in Borgueil. Gautier Audas in Nantes.

For sparkling wines
Ackerman, Gratien Meyer, Veuve Amiot in Saumur.

For Cremant de Loire
Lathéron at Amboise.

LESSER WINE-PRODUCING REGIONS OF FRANCE

France is a wine-drinking country; it is also a wine-producing country and whilst its reputation might be established by such famous names as Bordeaux and Burgundy, Champagne and the Rhône, if you draw a line from Nantes to Paris, wine is produced in almost every *département* to the south. Much of this is solely for family consumption, but a lot of it has also managed to create a reputation for itself within the hierarchy of French wine classification. Some of the wines are drunk entirely within the neighbourhood of their production; such a wine is the pride of Lorraine, for example – the thin, acid *vin gris* Côtes de Toul offered in every restaurant in Nancy and even benefiting from the status of VDQS. Many other wines have justifiably high reputations, which have often been built up over the centuries.

JURA

The great speciality of this historical vineyard area is the *vin jaune,* a dry fino-type wine made in the same way as the greatest sherries. A *flor* forms on the top of the wine, which is stored for several years in cask. This dries out the wine and concentrates the alcohol. The best-known village for it is Château-Chalon, followed by l'Etoile. The wine is sold in a traditional 50cl bottle, the *clavelin.*

Other curiosities includes a sweet dessert wine, the *vin de paille,* which is made from grapes that have been brought indoors and allowed to ripen on layers of straw; and *macvin,* a curious aperitif made in a similar fashion to port.

Of the more standard wines, the best is probably the rosé d'Arbois, which is reputed to be the best rosé after Tavel.

The area is dominated by one company, Henri Maire, which alone is responsible for the sale of about 60 per cent of the total production.

59

SAVOIE

All the wines from this region seem to be consumed by winter-sporters and very little is seen outside the area. The global Appellation Contrôlée Vin de Savoie encompasses a number of isolated pockets of vines from the shores of Lake Geneva, down to Aix-les-Bains and Chambéry. A vast number of grape varieties are used, notably the Jacquère and the Altesse for white wines and the Mondeuse for red wines, though the Gamay appears here and there.

The best wines from the region are Crépy, which is normally bottled with some residual gas, creating a lazily sparkling effect; and Seyssel, where both still wine and a Champagne-method sparkling wine are made. Varichon et Clerc are the major producers of the latter wine in this part of France.

LANGUEDOC-ROUSSILLON

The sea of vines from the Rhône to the Pyrenees has for long produced the lake of wine into which the French have been accustomed to dip their six-star bottles for everyday drinking. Now falling sales and competition from, notably, Italy, have meant that growers have had to improve their wines or go under. Of particular note are the efforts that have been made by a salt-producing company, les Salins du Midi, who have planted a variety of classical grapes along the Mediterranean coast, showing that with care very good wines can be made. Good red wines now come from the Fitou region and

Côtes du Roussillon, which have full AC status. At the VDQS level, good wines can be found in the Costières du Gard, Saint Chinian, Corbières and Minervois, where the Château de Gourgazaud is exceptional.

Generally speaking, the white wines in the region are disappointing, lacking the necessary acidity to keep them fresh. Blanquette de Limoux is a useful sparkling wine made by the Champagne method.

THE SOUTH-WEST

A look at a wine map of France shows that there is a considerable area under vines in the south-west of the country. Sadly, the majority of wine produced is not consumed as such but is distilled into Armagnac. There are, however, some notable wines produced in the region, of which perhaps the best-known is Cahors. Traditional methods of vinification and long ageing in cask have given the wine a deep colour, a slow maturation and the name of the 'black wine'. Modern commercial demands are changing this, but one is not surprised that for long it was used to 'soup up' the wines of Bordeaux. The Rigal family of the château at Parnach-Luzech produce good wines.

Not far to the north-west, adjoining the extremities of the vineyards of Bordeaux, are those of Bergerac. Here the best wines are sold under the names of Montravel (dry whites, similar to Entre-Deux-Mers) and Monbazillac (often described as the poor man's Sauternes).

In the valley of the River Tarn is produced the wine of Gaillac which, Hugh Johnson claims, must have earned its AC status on its past glories rather than on its present merits. Red, white, rosé and sparkling wines are produced.

Another historical wine is that of Jurançon, where a little excellent sweet white wine is made. However, the majority of the wine is now drier and has less distinction.

Other wines from the area include the heavy red wine of Madiran, the recent appellation of Côtes de Buzet, where a co-operative has a monopoly over the production and produces a range of wines similar in style to those of Bordeaux.

PROVENCE

There is little more pleasant than sitting on the quayside of some small harbour on the Mediterranean, drinking a well-chilled bottle of Provence rosé. Sadly, the same is not achieved on a cold winter's day in Wigan or Winnetka. Wines that are worth looking out for a bit further afield are the red wines of Bandol and the white wines of Cassis (where I have enjoyed the wines of La Ferme Blanche).

CORSICA

Since the French left Algeria, the wines of Corsica have improved considerably in quality. For modern tastes, they are perhaps rather high in alcohol, with the rosés generally showing best – after some time in an ice-bucket. The best wine comes from around Bastia and has the appellation Patrimonio.

PINEAU DES CHARENTES

I include this because I consider it to be one of the most underrated wines of France. It is made in the Cognac region, by adding cognac to unfermented grape juice. The result, when it is well-made, is a wonderful aperitif, slightly sweet at the beginning, but with a dry finish. My favourite pineau comes from J.-P. Ménard, who has a range of qualities.

Germany

Summary of Vineyard Register

Specific region (bestimmte Anbaugebiete)	Subregions (Bereich)	Large sites (Grosslagen)	Single Sites (Einzellage)	Communities (Gemeinde)
Rheinpfalz	2	26	335	170
Rheinhessen	3	24	446	167
Mosel-Saar-Ruwer	5	19	525	192
Baden	7	16	306	315
Württemberg	3	16	205	230
Nahe	2	7	321	80
Rheingau	1	10	120	28
Franken	3	17	155	125
Mittelrhein	3	11	112	59
Ahr	1	1	43	11
Hessische Bergstrasse	2	3	22	10
Total	32	150	2,590	1,387
Average size in hectares:	3,000	600	38 (at least 5)	70

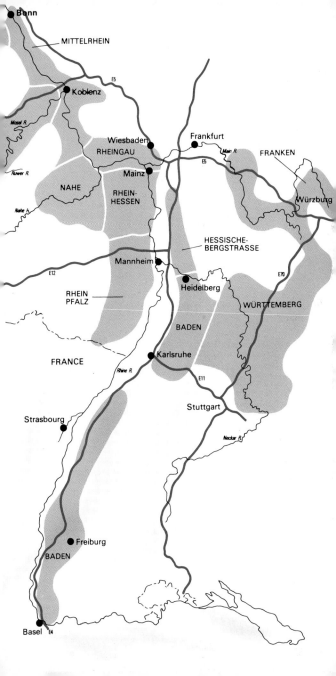

In the winding valleys of the rivers Ahr, Mosel, Saar, Ruwer, Rhine, Nahe, Main, Neckar and their tributaries, the world's most northerly wine-growing area, the natural conditions are enormously varied due to the different (micro) climates and soils. The nature of the soil is mainly slaty in the Mosel, Mittelrhein, but the Rhine districts have different types – clay, loess, marly soil, chalk, sand gravel, and loam. The vines are planted on a north-to-south axis to let the sun warm up the soil in the vineyard. The most common training system is the trellis type, except in the Mosel where every vine has its own stake. The climate is influenced by the river valleys, where the evaporation of the water in the river in summer or autumn causes a very good temperature balance. Also, the formation of fog helps to prevent frosts in spring and autumn.

The vineyards

The German vineyards are situated in Zone A of the European Economic Community's laws, except for Baden which is in Zone B. This division into zones is based on the different climates of the areas, and hence the alcoholic content of the wine. Although higher alcohol is produced in warmer climates, this does not relate to the quality of the wine.

The new German wine law of 1971 *(Weingesetz)* divides the vinelands into four table wine regions *(Tafelwein-Gebiete)* named after the rivers which flow through them. Quality wines *(Qualitätsweine)* grow in eleven designated regions *(bestimmte Anbaugebiete,* b. A). The specific regions are subdivided into districts *(Bereich),* villages and parts of villages, and their sites *(Lagen).* The site can consist of many vineyards *(Grosslagen)* where the soil and climate produce wines of similar character. An individual vineyard *(Einzellage)* must cover a minimum of 5 hectares, and may be owned by several growers. The wines may vary, depending on the growers, methods of cultivation and production. A wine can only be bottled under a vineyard name if at least 85 per cent of the wine comes from there.

Only a few large *Lagen* are in the hands of one owner, the biggest of these being the State Domain *(Steinberger).* There are currently five German State wine domains:

Verwaltung der Hessischen Staatsweinguter in Eltville; 196 hectares

Bayrische Landesanstalt für Wein-, Obst-, und Gartenbau, Hofkellerei, Würzburg; 186 hectares

Verwaltung der staatlichen Weinbaudomänen Trier;

Verwaltung der staatlichen Weinbaudomänen Niederhausen-Schloss Bökelheim;

Staatsweingut Meersburg am Bodensee.

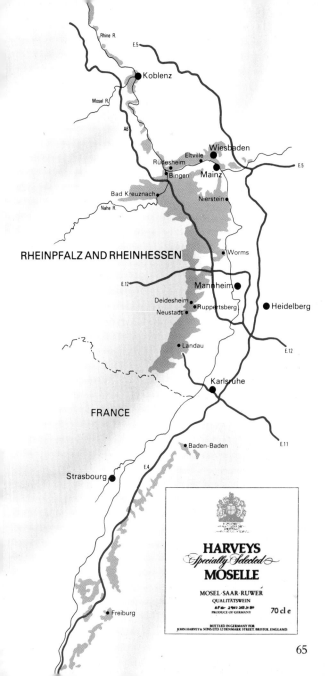

Rhine R.

E.5

● Koblenz

Mosel R.

A6

Wiesbaden

Eltville

Rüdesheim

Bingen   ● Mainz   E.5

Bad Kreuznach

Nahe R.   Nierstein

RHEINPFALZ AND RHEINHESSEN

● Worms

E.12

Mannheim ●

Deidesheim   ● Heidelberg

Ruppertsberg

Neustadt

● Landau   E.12

FRANCE

Karlsruhe

● Baden-Baden   E.11

E.4

Strasbourg ●

● Freiburg

HARVEYS
Specially Selected
MOSELLE

MOSEL · SAAR · RUWER
QUALITÄTSWEIN

AP Nr. 2 987 263 24 80
PRODUCE OF GERMANY   70 cl e

BOTTLED IN GERMANY FOR
JOHN HARVEY & SONS LTD 12 DENMARK STREET, BRISTOL, ENGLAND

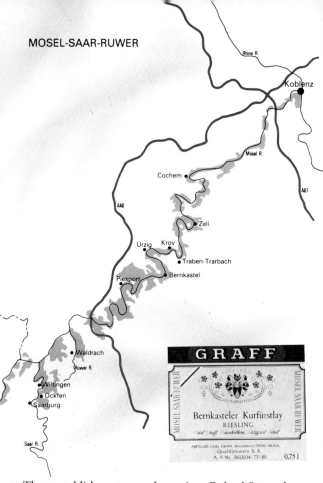

MOSEL-SAAR-RUWER

These establishments, run by various Federal States, have contributed a great deal to the reputation of German quality wines. Certain private wine estates, such as Schloss Johannisberg and Schloss Schönborn in Rheingau, also use the term 'domain'. The reason is that their owners were once independent rulers or persons of similar status, and the estate then had State functions and privileges. The viticultural section of the State instructional and experimental institutes in the Rhineland Palatinate are also called *Staatsweinguter,* meaning State wine domains.

All vineyards are entered in a vineyard register *(Weinberg Rolle),* and are carefully mapped with their boundaries – roads, footpaths, streams and so on.

There are about 100,000 families cultivating 90,000 hectares of vines, producing 1,170 million bottles, on average.

In the last few decades, the German wine growers' co-operatives have expanded enormously. The local co-operatives *(örtiche Genossenschaften)* sell most of their harvest to the regional central co-operative or, by choice, to private shippers and wholesalers. The six regional central co-operatives *(Zentralkellerein)* sell to the wholesale as well as the retail wine trade, and to restaurants.

Classification of wines

The new German wine law of 1971 *(Weingesetz)* has established three quality classes for wines, and also requires that the two superior classes are submitted to an official examination board *(amtliche Prüfung)*, in order to meet specific legal requirements.

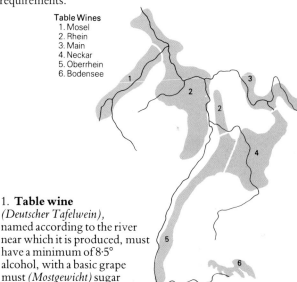

Table Wines
1. Mosel
2. Rhein
3. Main
4. Neckar
5. Oberrhein
6. Bodensee

1. **Table wine**
(Deutscher Tafelwein), named according to the river near which it is produced, must have a minimum of 8·5° alcohol, with a basic grape must *(Mostgewicht)* sugar content over 44° *Oechsle*.

2. **Quality controlled wine from a specific region** *(Qualitätswein bestimmter Anbaugebiete,* QbA), must carry a certification number and have a minimum of 60° *Oechsle*.

3. **Quality wine with predicate** *(Qualitätswein mit Prädikat* QmP) is superior quality controlled, and must also carry a certification number. QmP wines are subject to more rigorous harvest and quality controls, and are subdivided into degrees of sweetness *(Oechsle)*, as follows:

KABINETT The basic grade, with no chaptalization and a

67

minimum of 70° *Oechsle*. They are elegant, mature wines of better quality.

SPÄTLESE Means 'late harvest' and indicates rich, full-bodied wines made from ripe grapes with a minimum of 76° *Oechsle*.

AUSLESE All unripe grapes are rejected to give a special sweet wine with a minimum of 83° *Oechsle*.

BEERENAUSLESE Made only from over-ripe grapes affected by *botrytis cinerea*, with a minimum of 110° *Oechsle*.

TROCKENBEERENAUSLESE A selective picking of shrivelled grapes having the highest extract concentration, and a minimum of 150° *Oechsle*.

EISWEIN Produced from fully ripened grapes which have been frozen on the vine. They must be harvested at a maximum of -6° C. of frost. As the water in the grapes is frozen to ice, only the concentrate containing sugar and aroma is pressed out. These wines are a rarity because there is seldom frost at harvest time in the German wine regions.

Other wines are also divided into types:

LIEBFRAUMILCH The trade name for a wine which can only be produced in the Rheinhessen, Rheinpfalz, Nahe and Rheingau regions. It is a mild, pleasant wine which is popular in America and England but it can be rather uninteresting. It originated from the church of Worms known as Liebfrauen-stift. As Liebfraumilch is an invented name, no indication or origin can be mentioned on the label.

MOSELBLUEMCHEN This type of Mosel wine comes in a variety of qualities but generally as *Tafelweine*. It can be made in any part of the Mosel.

AFFENTHALER A red wine from Baden which is shipped in a monkey-embossed bottle. It originated in the Lichtental monastery in the Ave Valley ('Ave Thal') which gave its name to the village of Affenthal. Today, the village has been amalgamated with the next village, Eisenthal, and the name Affenthal has disappeared, though the name of the wine has been kept. It may be produced in all categories. Although it will not show a site name, the label can name the grape variety Pinot Noir *(Spätburgunder)*.

The label *(Etikett)*
    The label shows:
    The quality category (obligatory).
    The region for the quality wine of origin (obligatory).
    The *Bereich* or district.
    The geographical situation of the vineyards, which may

be the name of the village only or village and site name.
Grape varieties.
Grading of the wine, and degree of sweetness.
The vintage.
The producer (obligatory).

The most important factor introduced in the new German wine law *(Weingesetz)* is quality certification. Since 1971, all *Qualitätsweine* and *Qualitätsweine mit Prädikat* are quality tested: the harvest is inspected, the wine is analysed after it has been aged in the cellar and bottled, and experts taste it and grade it on a twenty-point system under official supervision. A national qualification number *(Amtliche Prüfnummer – A.P.Nr.)* is then allotted and shown on the label.

Wine Label 1975

RHEIN-HESSEN

1975 Niersteiner Gutes Domtal

Produced and bottled in Germany

„Sonnenhof"

6227 MITTELHEIM/RHEINGAU · W-GERMANY
W. ZAHN · WEINKELLEREI

A.P. Nr. 4 906 082 9 76

Qualitätswein b.A.

e.g. Wine Label 1975 A.P.Nr. 4. 906. 082. 9. 76.

76 Year of examination (not vintage year).	906 Number of the community where estate is situated.
4 Number of examining board.	082 Number of the Bottler.
	9 Bottler's current Number.

With the exception of table wines, application for the A.P.Nr. must be made for all wines and sekt (German sparkling wine) following bottling, and prior to their being offered for sale. If the flavour of the wine is not typical, the grape variety and vintage are not shown. The following information may also be shown on the label:

'dry' *(trocken)*
'semi-dry' *(halbtrocken)*
'suitable for diabetics' *(fur Diabetiker geeignet),* where details regarding the analysis are given. The bottle sometimes carries the yellow diabetic wine seal *(Diabetiker Weinsiegel)*
Quality seals and awards *(Deutsches Weinsiegel),* issued by national and regional wine awards, and the Baden seal.

Grape varieties

Most of the wine produced in Germany is white *(Weisswein)* made from white grapes. Pinot Noir and Portugieser are the main grape varieties used for making red wine *(Rotwein)*.

Rosé wines *(Roseewein)* are made from red grapes pressed as white wine. The colour particles are part of the inside skin of the grape, the flesh and juice are white. When the grapes are pressed immediately, the must is white or only slightly tinged with pink or grey. A rosé wine produced from only one kind of grape is known as *Weissherbst,* and the grape type must be stated on the label in the same print and size as the name *Weissherbst.*

Wines produced from mixed plantations of white and red grapes are called *Rotling.* The mixing or blending of white and red wine is prohibited and the grower must decide what he is going to do before the mash stage is passed. *Schillerwein* is a Rotling, made in Württemberg only, which is produced from a mixture of unfermented mash of white and red grapes or from red grapes only. This wine is pale red or pink.

Perlwein can be any of the wines named above. It contains effervescence caused by carbonic acid which does not exceed 2·5 atü at 20°C. Above this amount, it would become a sparkling wine. It is sold in ordinary bottles not champagne bottles. The three main grape varieties *(Rebsorten)* which are planted in three-quarters of Germany's vineyard are Riesling, Müller-Thurgau and Sylvaner. The Riesling, which ripens late with small grapes and requires a good warm position and good soil, produces some of the best quality wines, especially if gathered late *(Spätlese)* and from selected grapes *(Auslese).* These are flowery, full bodied and round wines, with a characteristic spicy bouquet and flavour. The Sylvaner ripens earlier, producing a mellow, soft wine with a rather neutral flavour. Müller-Thurgau is mainly planted in the poorer vineyards, and makes a light, pleasantly smooth and slightly muscatel wine which should be drunk when it is young.

The wines

There are eleven designated quality wine regions *(Qualitäts-Anbaugebiete).*

RHEINPFALZ

The Palatinate, which is about 86 kilometres long and 30 kilometres wide, is Germany's biggest vineyard area. It is situated just north of Alsace, under the shelter of the continuation of the Vosges mountains called the Haardt. The Riesling is at its best in the Mittel-Haardt at the vineyards of Hohesburg; Geisböhl; Deidesheim; Forst, where some of

Germany's best known wine comes from; Jesuitengarten; Kirchenstück; Freundstück; and Wachenheim. The wines are rich in body and bouquet, aromatic and spicy, ranging from fresh carafe type to full flavoured wines.

RHEINHESSEN

Covering an area of 22,000 hectares, this region is well protected by the Taunus, Hunsrueck and Haardt mountain ranges which surround it. A great variety of wines are produced, ranging from table wines to the most exquisite wines. Although the Sylvaner has been made famous at Worms for the commercial production of Liebfraumilch, the Riesling comes into its own at the towns of Nierstein, with 300 large wine estates; Oppenheim; and Nackenheim. Well known vineyards of the region are Hipping, Pettenthal, and Rothenberg. These wines are aromatic, round, and flowery, with a well-balanced fragrant bouquet, and the Rieslings are elegant and racy.

NAHE

The region covers an area of 4,500 hectares with an average annual yield of 400,000 hectolitres, produced by some eighty-three wine-growing communities. The best known growers are situated around the spa town of Bad Kreuznach, the wine capital with its State institute of wine-growing. The Riesling grown here produces a grapey, full-flavoured wine. At the foot of the red mountain *(Rotenfelser)* which is 200 metres high, the vineyards are well sheltered and face south. Some better-known wines come from the copper mine *(Kupfergrube)* on the eastern limit of the village of Schlossbockelheim; their taste is reminiscent of blackcurrants.

MITTELRHEIN

The Riesling and Sylvaner grow on quartzite and Devonian slate in this region, north of the Rheingau, producing wines of medium quality, with a pronounced fruity, very robust Riesling. Most of the wines are drunk locally. The well known sites are at Siebengebirge Konigswinter, Rheinburgengau, Boppard, and Bacharach.

MOSEL-SAAR-RUWER

Situated along the winding steep banks of slaty soil, this region is well suited for the Riesling. The slabs of slate in the vineyard allow good drainage and also trap the warmth of the sun. The vineyards mainly face south. The most famous areas are Kasel, Waldrach in the Ruwer, Wiltingen in the Saar, Trittenheim, Bernkastel, and Piesport in the Mosel. Although they have a low alcohol content, the wines have a pleasant, refreshing, light acidity, often showing a slight effervescence *(Spritzig)*.

RHEINGAU
The cluster of vineyards on the right bank of the Rhine, which at this point flows from east to west, face south and are well protected by the wooded Taunus mountains. The Riesling planted in the slaty soil of these slopes produces a fruity wine which blends ideally with its fine sweetness. The sunny and moist climate encourages the 'noble rot' as the grapes ripen. The larger estates are situated in Hochheim, Hattenheim, Winkel, Erbach Kiedrich, Eltville, Rüdesheim, Johannisberg, Hallgarten, Assmannshausen and of course the wine school at Geisenheim which owns 40 hectares of vines. A famous red wine from the Blauer Spätburgunder (Pinot Noir) grape is produced at Assmannshausen, which has a slight characteristic flavour of almonds, and varies in colour according to the maturity of the grapes from a bright fiery red to a rich dark garnet hue.

HESSISCHE BERGSTRASSE
Known as the spring garden *(Fruehlingsgarten)* of Germany, this region is a magnificent sight when the cherry and other fruit trees are in full blossom. The climate is very mild, ideal for the Müller-Thurgau, Riesling and Sylvaner grapes. There are two *Bereiche,* Starkenburg and Umstadt. Heppenheim at the centre has a historic cellar in the Kurmainzer Amtshof. The best wine is the Heppenheimer Steinkopf, generally known as Steinkopfer. The wines show a fresh, fruity character and should be drunk young, but the best ones can age a little.

BADEN
The best vineyards are in the Kaiserstuhl, where the Pinot Gris grape *(Ruländer)* produces a fruity, flowery and spicy white wine, which can range from dry to sweet depending on the vintage. The red wine from the Pinot Noir of Burgundy fame *(Spätburgunder),* makes a light and pleasant summer drink. South of the Kaiserstuhl at Markgräflerland, a white wine is produced from the Chasselas grape of Swiss fame *(Gutedel).* Near the lake of Konstanz, at Meersburg, a pink tinted wine *(Seewein)* is made from the Pinot Noir.

WÜRTTEMBERG
This area does not suit every kind of grape – it has poor climate and the soils are shell limestone, red marl, and bituminous marl, so the vineyards have to be planted carefully for the wines to achieve their own particular characteris-

tics. There is, for instance, the Sylvaner in the Kocher valley and Tauber valley, the Trollinger and Limberger grapes in the Heilbronn district, the Black Riesling in the Lauffen region on the Neckar, the Riesling in the Rems valley and on the slopes of the Burgberg, and the Schemelberg near Weinsberg. More red wine than white is produced from the Trollinger, and most of it is handled by large co-operatives. Heilbronn is the main wine-growing area, where vines extend into the capital city of Stuttgart.

FRANKEN

The vineyard here is situated on very steep slopes, and the soil, basically red marl, produces good mature wines. All the quality wines are bottled in an exclusive flask-shaped *Bocksbeutel* bottle. Famous wines come from the capital district of Wurzburg at the vineyards of Stein and Leiste. The wine is full-bodied and contains the highest extract of all the northern wine-growing areas. At best, it resembles a white Burgundy.

AHR

The most northerly vineyard extending 25 kilometres over slate mountains, producing a fresh, racy Riesling wine and red wines from Spätburgunder and Portugieser grapes. Some Müller-Thurgau is also planted, and this makes a milder wine. Well known vineyards are Ahrweiler, Bachem, Bad Neuenahr and May Schoss, which is also known for its red sekt.

Sekt

This name is reserved for quality controlled sparkling wine. The lower grade is known as Schaumwein, which literally means 'foaming wine'. Schaumwein is manufactured from grape must. The end product must contain carbonic acid as a result of alcoholic fermentation and a minimum of 8·85 per cent by volume alcohol. The best method used is the *méthode champenoise*. There are three classified types of German sparkling wine: *Inländischer Schaumwein* (ordinary); *Sekt* (quality controlled); *Deutscher Sekt bestimmter Anbaugebiete* (b.A) (higher class) made only from German Quality wines. In order to qualify for the denomination as Sekt, it must: contain a minimum of 10 grams actual alcohol; be produced by second fermentation and without the addition of carbonic acid; remain at least sixty days (or three weeks if in containers) on the lees, and be stored for a minimum of nine months under the carbonic pressure of 3·5 atü at 20°C.

It has to pass the various tests for allocation of a national qualification number.

Italy

SWITZERLAND

Aosta

Milan

Turin

Asti

Genoa

Trento

Verona

Padua

Venice

Trieste

Parma

Modena

Bologna

Ravenna

Pisa

Florence

Siena

Perugia

Assisi

Macerata

Grosseto

L'Aquila

Rome

Frascati

Fiuggi

Palermo

Messina

Marsala

Syracuse

Adige R.

Po R.

Arno R.

Tiber R.

Collio

Denominazione di origine controllata

Tocai Friulano

SCHIOPETTO

Imbottigliato all'origine dalla
Azienda Agricola Mario Schiopetto

CAPRIVA DEL F. - ITALIA

13% VOL.   0,720ℓ

Though Italy is barely half the size of France, it is the world's largest producer of wine. Its average annual production is 7·85 million hectolitres and this is despite a very large proportion of the country being mountainous, with the Alps in the north and the Appenines stretching like a backbone down to Italy's toe. The rich alluvial soils of the great river valleys produce vast quantities of wine of very ordinary quality and Italy must look to the hillsides at the foot of the Alps and to the Tuscan hills to support its claim that it can produce really great wines.

The Italians are also the largest consumers of wine per head of adult population in the world and it is this, above all, which gives them a familiar and rather casual attitude to wine. It is simply taken for granted and, in consequence, many methods of winemaking are slapdash in the extreme. Most wine drinkers in non-producing countries cut their vinous teeth on French and German classics and judge the wines of other countries by those yardsticks. By the same token, Italian food is more robust than delicate, when compared to the *haute cuisine* of France, and it may be unjust to condemn the style of Italian wines, developed by countless generations of winegrowers and makers because of ideas preconceived elsewhere.

Classification of wines

The foundations of the Italian wine laws were laid in Tuscany, where the use of the name Chianti was fast getting completely out of hand. In 1963 the Government gave official blessing to the idea and three years later the first DOC (Denominazione di Origine Controllata) regulations began to take effect.

The DOC regulations are in some ways less rigid than the French Appellation Contrôlée laws. The prime movers are the local Consorzio (wine growers organisations) in a semi-official association with the regional or national agricultural authorities. The system is slowly beginning to work and influence the quality of the wines. At the time of writing 209 wines can be granted the accolade and a higher tier, DOCG (Denominazione di Origine Controllata e Garantita), is in the process of being introduced. The laws embrace the district of origin, the grape varieties permitted, yield per hectare, methods of production and ageing, and alcoholic strength; in most regions, a quality control tasting is also required. There is no doubt that a great advance has been made, but the wines certainly suffer from an inflexibility in the required time for being kept in wood.

The nomenclature of Italian wines often seems deliberately contrived to confuse. Some derive their names from a geographical region and others from the variety of vine, sometimes qualified by a district name. In Piedmont, for instance, Barolo and Barbaresco are districts, while Barbera is a grape. Elsewhere it becomes even more confusing; for example, Montepulciano is a town in Tuscany, and a grape name in Abruzzo.

The Consorzio deserves recognition for what it has done, as it was often able to act in areas where officials remained indifferent.

PIEDMONT

As with a page of print, the top left-hand corner is a good place to start to look at Italian wine. The Piedmont region is the home of the greatest, if not the best-known, Italian wines. It is in the north-west, the nearest region to France, and spreads through the foothills of the Alps. The vineyards are on the same latitude as much of the Rhône valley and, indeed, Bordeaux itself. The greatest industrial city of Turin marks the northern limit of the area. South of this stretch the Langhe and the Monferrato Hills and the finest vineyards are on their south-western flanks in the province of Cuneo. These vineyards are centred on the local wine capital, Alba, which is an oasis of gastronomy and home of the famous white truffles.

Grape varieties

The Nebbiolo is planted in the Alba district, and other red
grape varieties, after which wines are named, are Barbera,
Grignolino, Dolcetto and Freisa. All these can be qualified by
the name of the districts from which they come, e.g. Barbera
d'Alba, Dolcetto di Dogliana and Grignolini d'Asti. No
grapes are exclusive to one district, all have their DOC's and
the nomenclature can become extremely complicated.

NORTH-WEST ITALY

Valle d'Aosta
1. Enfer D'Arvier
2. Donnaz

Liguria
9. Cinque Terre
Cinque Terre Sciacchetra
10. Rossese di Dolceaqua

Piedmont
7. Barbera D'Alba, Barolo
8. Barbera D'Asti
Bonarda
Gavi
Asti Spumante
Barbaresco
Moscato
Nebbiolo d'Alba
3. Ghemme
Sizzano
Gattinara
4. Boca
5. Carema
6. Erbaluce di Caluso
PIEMONTE – 36 DOC'S

Lombardy
11. Colli Tortonesi
12. Franciacorta Rosso
13. Botticino
14. Bardolino
15. Riviera del Garda
16. Valtellina
LOMBARDY – 12 DOC'S

Barolo and Barbaresco

To the south and north, respectively, of Alba are wines named after the villages of Barolo and Barbaresco. The wines are close cousins, both red and made from the Nebbiolo grape. Barolo is the senior partner with a minimum alcohol content of 13°, against Barbaresco's 12·5°· They are full, warm and robust but have a certain austerity, possibly due to the statutory time they must spend in wood before bottling. When the DOC laws were formulated much emphasis was placed on this ageing and often it seems excessive, but without it the wines lose the right to the denomination. Barbaresco can be sold after two years but Barolo has to wait for three. No amount of argument will persuade the growers that the wines might appeal to a wider market if bottled earlier to retain an extra fruitiness.

Both districts are pioneers in the field of the upper tier of the DOC system and can achieve the status of DOCG. As in other DOC areas, the respective Consorzio issue their numbered slip labels as an extra voluntary sign of authenticity – for Barolo a golden lion and the tower of Barbaresco castle for its neighbour, both on blue fields.

Asti

Asti is known throughout the world for its Spumante, a popular half-sweet sparkling wine produced from the Muscatel grape. A still version, Moscato (Naturale) d'Asti, is one of the few white wines likely to be seen outside the region. A small amount of Malvasia is also planted, confusingly producing red wine.

Grinzane

In the Barolo region at Grinzane is a 14th century castle, once the home of Cavour, and now housing a wine museum and an exceptional restaurant serving local specialities and representative wines from throughout Piedmont. It is a very good centre from which to study the wines and the complexities of their DOCs. Many individual growers bottle their own wines, which are available for comparative tasting in the castle's *enoteca*.

It is an area of autumn mists which swirl around the valley, leaving the hilltop castles and estates in sunshine, like islands in the sea. These vineyards are the most favoured, and such estates are often distinguished by the prefix Bricco, the "Premiers Crus" of Barolo and Barbaresco.

Gavi

The most important white wine of Piedmont is from Gavi in the province of Allessandria in the south of the region. The vineyards, at around 300 metres altitude, are planted exclusively with Cortese vines (the DOC is interchangeable between Gavi or Cortese di Gavi), giving a pale wine that is crisp, fresh and quite dry. Sometimes the wines seem a little bland and there is an affinity to the Chenin wines of the Loire, including an attractive, slightly bitter aftertaste. Vinification has been improved in recent years and one of the most interesting Italian sparkling wines is also made here, by the Champagne method.

Some other wines from north-west Italy

It is a puzzle why it took so long for the great wines of Piedmont to become known outside Italy and the probable explanation is that because the region is locked in by mountains to the north, west and south, their only way to the outside world was through the Valley of the Po river flowing eastwards to the Adriatic. Tuscan wines, on the other hand, had access through Leghorn to the western Mediterranean trade routes. But this isolation from other wine-growing areas gave the wines their individual characteristics and the growers a reluctance to change their methods.

An outcrop of vineyards planted with the Nebbiolo vine is found north of the autostrada between Turin and Milan on the way to Lake Maggiore. The grape, which in this area is known as the Spanna, is taken less seriously than in Piedmont and is, therefore, often more appealing to outsiders unaccustomed to the austerity of wines kept overlong in wood. Much is found under the varietal label of Spanna and others, named for their districts, are Gattinara, Ghemme, Sizzano and Boca, deserving recognition as some of the best wines of Piedmont.

There are two satellite winemaking areas bordering Piedmont – to the north, the French-speaking Val d'Aosta, and in the south, Liguri on the Mediterranean coast between the French frontier and La Spezia. These attractive wines are seldom seen outside their districts but are of more than passing interest to holidaymakers in the two popular tourist areas.

LOMBARDY
The Valtellina

Continuing north-east, beyond Milan and Lake Como, in the Lombardy region is the Valtellina, a district of spectacular terraced vineyards clinging to the mountainsides with cables to bring the grapes down to the valleys at vintage time. The area is centred on the town of Sondrio, and the Nebbiolo grape is the aristocrat of the district – the DOCs are Grumello, Sassello, and the interestingly named Inferno.

They are full, firm, robust reds, often seemingly kept over-long in wood, with very little to distinguish one from another. Nino Negri is the great grower of the area, though now rather submerged in a Swiss-Italian consortium. Here, too, is a vinous curiosity – Sfursat made from grapes picked and concentrated by being hung indoors on wires until pressed at Christmas time. It has a kinship with the Reciotos of the Veneto.

ALTO ADIGE

An intrepid traveller can continue north-eastwards, crossing the Alps by the Stelvio pass where Italy, Switzerland and Austria meet, and dropping down again into the south Tyrol, which the Italians prefer to call the Alto Adige. It seems almost a no-man's land, Italian in name since ceded by the Austrians after the First World War but extremely Germanic in character – indeed, most of the region's wines are exported northwards over the Brenner Pass. A latent nationalism justifies the Austrians describing the wines, when sold in their country, as produce of Austria and the names of the wines are transcribed in Italian or German according to the direction in which they are to travel – this dual naming can be very confusing.

In Bolzano, or perhaps Bolzen, an Italian who asks directions in his own language will not get an answer, but the wines are among the best in Italy.

The Alto Adige is, in fact, only half a region as the Trentino province, taking its name from the town of Trento, has been tacked on at the south to give a numerical balance between the Italian and German speaking populations. This may have political advantages but the division still exists and is re-flected in the wines of the region and a lack of consistency in their labelling.

Therefore, when dealing with the wines it is better to consider the region in two parts.

Classification of wines

It may be that the Germanic influence brought a better sense of order to things in the Alto Adige. There is an abundance of small growers but a large part of the production is handled by well-organized co-operatives – Cantina Sociale or Win-zergenossenschaften. The vineyards follow the valley of the Adige southwards from Merano, with branches into the valleys of the river's tributaries, and the wine names are divided almost equally between districts and grape varieties, the latter often being old friends from Germany or France. Many are a cross between the two; a district qualified by the name of the grape. Most frequently seen are the generic wines with the simple DOC of Alto Adige or, in German, Südtirol.

Grape varieties

The white vines planted include Sylvaner, Riesling Italico (Welsch riesling); Riesling Renano (Rhine-riesling – the classic grape of Germany and Alsace); various Sylvaner-Riesling crosses, such as the Müller-Thurgau; and the Traminer Aromatico (Gewürztraminer), which the locals claim is named from the village of Tramin about halfway between Bolzano and Trent. Those with a French connection are Pinot Bianco (Weissburgunder), Pinot Grigio (Rülander) and Sauvignon. There is also a sprinkling of Muscatel derivatives (Moscato or Muskatella). These are sweet wines, while the others are predominantly dry. The red wines can be made from the Cabernet, Merlot and Pinot Nero (Blauburgunder) and two regional specialities, the Schiava (Vernatschs) and Lagrein.

The wines

All of the white wines are dry except for the Muscatel derivatives, which are sweet. As for the reds, their Bordelais and Burgundian ancestry is recognizable in the wine made from the French grapes, but those from the local twins are interesting in their own right, full of fruit, warm and generous and with a slight almondy bitterness at the back. An outstanding rosé, with as much colour as many reds, is made from the Lagrein Rosato (Lagrein Kretzer). The wines are not over-alcoholic – mostly between 11° and 11·5°, and the Schiava is often even lighter. There is also a mawkish half-sweet pink Muscatel (Rosenmuskateller), which is best avoided.

A cut above the generics are wines with more closely defined orgins, notably Santa Maddalena (St Magdalener), from just north of Bolzano, and Lago di Caldaro or Caldaro (Kalterersee or Kalterer) from the shores of a lake south-west of the city. Here the Schiava really comes into its own (a small addition of foreign grapes is permitted) and provides the most individual and attractive wines of the area. An exclusively white DOC is Terlano (Terlaner), upstream from Bolzano, a wine made predominantly from the Pinot Bianco but with a healthy tolerance of grapes from the other Alto Adige varieties.

TRENTINO

There is no official division between the Alto Adige and Trentino districts, but there is an immediately recognizable change in atmosphere.

Grape varieties

The German nomenclatures disappear as the river flows southwards, the Riesling (both Italico and Renano) and Traminer Aromatico remain, but the Schiava has been left behind in the vineyards higher up the valley. Although the Lagrein survives as a permitted variety, the most significant red grapes are the Cabernet, Merlot and Pinot Nero, while the Pinot Bianco and Pinot Grigio complete the range of whites.

The wines

There has been great improvement in the wines in recent years, largely due to the encouragement and technological assistance of Cavit, a sort of co-operative of co-operatives, a giant organization which draws wine from all the Cantine Sociale in the district. Cavit was one of the pioneers of the 2-litre bottle, which typifies Italian wines on the supermarket shelves throughout the Common Market, but they themselves have maintained remarkably high quality standards.

The wines reach the consumers under any number of labels but the Merlot and Cabernet can be outstanding and the white wines – the Pinot Grigio possibly having the edge on the Bianco – manage to achieve a balance of fruit and crispness rarely found so far south. Most wines from this southern section of the region are content with the generic DOC of Trentino, usually followed by the varietal name. There is a considerable industry in sparkling wine, almost all made by the *charmat, cuve close* or tank method but, because of the influence of the Pinot grape, among the most attractive in Italy.

FRIULI-VENEZIA-GIULIA

After its post-war vicissitudes, Trieste is again an Italian city, but it is at the end of a corridor between the Adriatic and Yugoslavia. Lying to the north is the town of Gorizia, the Yugoslav border dictating which part of the conurbation is Goriče, and from here to the west and north-west are some of the most interesting vineyards in Italy.

Grape varieties

The Yugoslav Riesling, now correctly Welsch- or Laskiriesling (being anything but the Rhine-riesling of the EEC) comes from immediately across the frontier but the inherent independence and enterprise of the Italians is apparent in the style and individuality of the Friuli wines.

Nowadays, with one exception, the vines are old friends from elsewhere but the region is blessed with serious and

innovative growers who have made striking improvements
in quality in the last few years. It may be that they ape their
masters, but, for a wine drinker with preconceived ideas,
they come very close to their French or German prototypes.
The latitude of the region is north of that of Bordeaux and the
Merlot and Cabernet (both Cabernet Franc and Cabernet
Sauvignon are planted) can be outstanding, but a gentle
relaxation of the DOC regulations to allow judicious blend–

NORTH-EAST ITALY

Trentino Alto Adige
1. Meranese de Collina Terlano
2. Santa Maddalena
3. Traminer
4. Merlot
   Pinot Nero
   Cabernet
   Teroldego Rotaliano
   Riesling
   Marzemino
5. Trentino
TRENTINO – 11 DOC'S

Veneto
6. Bardolino Classico
7. Bardolino Superiore
8. Breganze
9. Soave, Valpolicella
10. Colli Berici
    Gambellara
11. Colli Euganei
12. Tocai del Piave
    Menot del Piave
    Cabernet del Piave
    Prosecco
13. Prosecco di Conegliano
    Valdobbiadene
14. Cabernet di Pramaggiore
VENETO – 16 DOC'S

Friuli-Venezia Giulia
15. Colli Orientali
    Riesling
    Tocai
    Sauvignon
    Merlot
    Grave del Friuli
16. Collio Goriziano
17. Picolit
18. Lambrusco
FRIULI – 6 DOC'S

83

ing of the two, as in Bordeaux itself, might produce wines of better balance.

White wines are made from the Riesling Renano (the good one!), Pinot Bianco and Pinot Grigio and Tocai – this last a subject of some discussion as in Alsace Tokay is considered synonymous with Pinot Gris – and some experimental plantings of Sauvignon. The wines have about 12° alcohol but careful vinification preserves their fruit and freshness.

Classification of wines

The DOCs can be extremely complicated with many combinations of districts and varietals. Collio Goriziano, from a range of hills right on the Yugoslav border, is probably the most distinguished district, but complicates the issue by being permitted to drop Goriziano.

The word 'colli' means hillside and the Colli Orientali del Friuli is a good DOC usually quantified by the grape varieties, as are those from the Grave del Friuli – as the name suggests, this is a district where the vineyards are on gravelly, well-drained soil.

Picolit

Colli Orientali is also the home of one of Italy's vinous curiosities, Picolit. The local protagonists aver that it was once as highly acclaimed as Château d'Yquem. It is a white wine of extraordinary concentration, often achieving a natural alcohol content of 15° with considerable residual sugar. It is a wine to be sipped slowly and has a strange haunting underlying taste. There is no other wine quite like it, but it is so rare as to be approaching the esoteric.

THE VENETO
Verona

It is something of a relief to come back to earth in the Veneto. although the region stretches from Lake Garda to east of Venice and through a corridor touching the Austrian border south to the River Po, serious wine interest is confined to an area 25 kilometres east and west of Verona.

Bardolino

The little town of Bardolino on the shore of Lake Garda gives its name to one of Italy's great red wines. It lacks the potential to develop which can be found in the greater wines of Piedmont but is often more immediately attractive.

The predominant vine variety is the Corvina Veronese which, as its name suggests, is a local speciality. Up to 25 per cent of Rondinella is also used and other varieties are permitted in relatively small quantities.

The lake itself certainly has a moderating influence on the vineyards and Bardolino can be criticized for lacking concentration, but it is a wine of undisputed charm and incomparable in the beautiful lakeside country of its birthplace.

As elsewhere in Italy, the boundaries of the production area had stretched before the arrival of the DOC regulations and there is both Bardolino Classico from the heartland on the lake shore and Bardolino *tout court* from the hills between there and the Adige river. The alcoholic minimum is 10·5° but Superiore status can be achieved with 11·5° and an extra year of ageing, neither adding anything to a wine whose main attributes are lightness and the fruitiness of youth. The wine is often fermented in contact with the skins for only a few hours; the resulting attractive dark rosé is known as Bardolino Chiaretto.

Valpolicella and Valpantena

Immediately across the Adige and north-west of Verona is Valpolicella Classico. Here again the boundary stretchers have done their work, the fringe area expanding eastwards far beyond the city. The grape varieties and their proportions are the same as Bardolino, but Valpolicella is usually a wine of much more substance and concentration, although the alcohol minimum is also the same at 11°. Again, there is provision for a Superiore despite a consensus that youth and lightness are definite assets. Within the Bardolino area is the valley of Valpantena whose wines are entitled to a DOC of their own.

There are many Cantine Sociale supplying the big shipping houses, but these red wine districts also abound with serious small growers who have a great pride in their wines and a hospitality to match.

As with the Sfursat in Valtellina, there is inordinate local enthusiasm for Recioto, a curiosity achieved by hanging the grape bunches indoors for several months after the vintage and vinifying them when half-dried and containing an extra concentration of sugar. Usually some unfermented sugar remains, making the wine particularly mawkish to strangers, but sometimes the wine ferments completely, resulting in an extremely alcoholic but quite dry wine known as Amarone. Inevitably, in the process it becomes partially oxidized and should be treated with circumspection.

Soave

The third area of the district produces the best-known Italian white wine. Soave Classico is centred on a small town west of Verona with a larger area on its periphery. Small proprietors making their own wine do exist, but a very large proportion of the production is made in the enormous, but modern and efficient co-operative cellar. This means that Soave, while always sound and well-made, has been reduced to a lowest common denominator and there is an inescapable feeling that somewhere around the corner is a wine of more individuality and interest. Nonetheless, it is Italy's most reliable commercial white wine – pale, light, dry and crisp. It is important to drink it as young as possible and even the 'Superiore' qualification commendably requires only six months age before sale. There is a Recioto which is popular and, being white, can be enjoyed with fruit or other desserts. The predominant grape (up to 90 per cent) is Garganega, and the balance is Trebbiano di Soave.

Classification of wines
All the DOC wines of the Veronese district are entitled to bear a numbered neck label issued by the Consorzio Tutela Vino. There is a variation for Classico wines and those without a vintage year, but the label common to most has a gold background with a bishop, complete with crook, sitting on his throne by the lakeside.

Other vineyards in Veneto
There are many other vineyards in Veneto, but two which are of some note are on hillsides south of Vicenza and west of Padua – Colli Berici and Colli Euganei respectively. A third is in the lower part of the valley of the Piave, which eventually flows into the Venice lagoon. The denominations of the first and last are qualified by the name of the grape from which they are made, while the Euganei hill wines settle for being Rosso or Bianco, from a hotchpotch of grapes, or Moscato, all of which can also be sparkling. Much finds its way to the cafés and restaurants of Venice, where Osbert Sitwell once heard an American lady tourist ask a waiter for the same good wine as she had enjoyed the previous year, adding, 'I think it was made from grapes'.

EMILIA-ROMAGNA
South of Veneto is Emilia-Romagna, a region of mixed gastronomic blessings. Bologna has inspired the sauce for countless plates of pasta and Parma has provided parmesan cheese to grate over myriad Italian dishes, and incomparable hams famous throughout the world. Why, then, should the wine be so undistinguished?
The broad valley of the Po, which flows through the region, is one of the most fertile and productive areas in the world and rich soil is anathema to wine. Quantity and quality have never gone together, and quantity is the order of the day in

the case of Lambrusco. The grape is grown throughout the region and only a proportion of the wine claims (or seeks) a DOC. Much of it is exported but, fortunately, very little comes to Britain. It is red, sweet, and usually sparkling.

TUSCANY

Immediately to the south and west of Emilia-Romagna is the region of Tuscany, the home of Chianti, the best known of all Italian red wines. Here too are the ancient republics of Florence, Siena and Pisa. The patronage of the Medicis and later Grand Dukes and other noblemen of Florence extended to agriculture in all forms and, from earliest times, the country estates of these nobles were famous for their wines.

CENTRAL ITALY

ITALY

Much is known about the early history of wine growing in the province from the writing of the time, and many names from mediaeval times can be identified with the Tuscan wines of today.

Grape varieties
The predominant grape throughout the Chianti region is Sangiovese, with admixtures of Canaiolo and smaller quantities of two white grapes – Trebbiano and the local strain of Malvasia.

Chianti Classico
The Chianti region is divided into several districts, but Chianti Classico, the central area, is considered to be the best. In the first half of the 19th century Baron Beltino Ricasoli, later Prime Minister of Italy, started a series of experiments at his Castle of Brolio with the intention of improving Tuscan wines, and his efforts undoubtedly established the reputation of Chianti.

His descendants still make wine at Brolio, which is one of the leading Chianti Classico estates.

Unfortunately, however, Baron Ricasoli's efforts to popularize Chianti led to exploitation by other winemakers as the demand for the wine grew. The boundaries were stretched and 'Chianti', sold in distinctive rush-covered flasks, became virtually the generic wine name of the region. Sadly, many wine areas, at least as old as Chianti, were submerged in this bursting of the banks and are only just beginning to reassert themselves.

Classification of Chianti wines
The Chianti consorzio is one of the oldest and was a pioneer in the establishment of some of the earliest DOCs in 1967. A compromise was reached and the original vineyard area, taking the name from the Chianti hills over which ran the ancient road from Florence to Siena, was designated 'Chianti Classico'. These wines have a necklet bearing a black cockerel. Other wines, which had to come from the quality wine-producing areas, kept the straightforward denomination, 'Chianti', and have a necklet showing a 'putto' or cherub.

Within the broad Chianti area are smaller DOCs with district suffixes. The best-known of these, each with their own necklets, are: Colline, Pisane, Montalbano, Colli Fiorentini, Rufina, Colli Aretini, and Colli Senesi. All these wines are of appreciably greater quality than most wines labelled 'Chianti'. Many estates in these districts claim to be more ancient and at least the equal of Chianti Classico. One, within

88

Chianti Montalbano, has declared complete independence dropping the Chianti prefix altogether and obtaining its own DOC in 1975. This is Carmignano, a small hill town north-west of Florence, where a proportion of Cabernet vines are now planted, making a distinctive attractive wine well able to stand on its own.

South of Siena, within the Chianti Colli Sinesi DOC area, are two other very notable red wines. Production is small and the wines are scarce enough in Italy itelf. They have consequently acquired something of a rarity value (and price) and can be a disappointment when eventually encountered. The Chianti grape, Sangiovese, under different local names, is predominant in both districts. The wines have earned a place in the wine aristocracy of Italy and the lesser of the two, Vino Nobile di Montepulciano, even advertises the fact in its name. The grapes are grown at up to 600 metres on the hills, surrounding the ancient and beautiful mountain town of Montepulciano. In youth, it is fairly tough, tannic wine but it can be very impressive when old.

At Montalcino, another mountain township 25 kilometres to the west, the Sangiovese is known as the Brunello, and Brunello di Montalcino has an even greater reputation than Vino Nobile di Montepulciano, but sometimes suffers from being kept overlong in wood – four years is the compulsory minimum under its DOC regulation. It is the bigger, more concentrated, wine of the two, with an alcoholic minimum of 12·5°· The estates are small, the owners dedicated and the wine potentially one of the best in Italy.

All these DOCs can be 'declassified' to Chianti and many of the less successful ones often are, which helps maintain the quality.

White wines

A large quantity of pleasant dry white wine is made in the region, mostly from Trebbiano grapes. Most Chianti estates produce a white companion which can only be sold as Vino di Tavola di Toscano, but Vernaccia di San Gimignano deserves a mention, if only for the glory of its birthplace, a wonderful mediaeval town on the western fringe of the Chianti Classico area.

CENTRAL ITALY

To all intents and purposes, serious winemaking peters out as a move is made southwards into Umbria and Latium and the Marches, on the Adriatic coast. It is true that many are world famous, but this is mainly due to their names being easy to pronounce and remember by the tourists who flock to Rome. Most are white and vary from medium dry to unashamedly sweet – Orvieto, Frascati and the enthusiastically named Est! Est!! Est!!! Romance comes into it somewhere and only rarely are the wines, made from the Trebbiano grape, more than agreeable and refreshing.

Along the Adriatic coast – in the Marches – are wines made mainly from the Verdicchio grape. They are usually dry and sometimes include a district name: Verdicchio dei Casteli di Jesi is the best known. For some reason, the labels on the fancy shaped bottles have pseudo-Greek lettering.

A large quantity of ordinary red wine is made throughout the three regions and mostly consumed anonymously in carafes by the Romans.

SOUTHERN ITALY

It would be nice to believe that the hills around the bay of Naples produce wine as beautiful as the countryside itself but, alas, this is anything but the case. Lachryma Christi has a memorable name but little else to offer. There is even uncertainty as to the colour of the tears – serious opinion favours white wine only, but rosé and red wines claim the name with equanimity. Such are the rivalries and doubts in the district, on the slopes of Mount Vesuvius, that one of Italy's most famous wine names has made little progress along the road to DOC entitlement.

There are many other red and white wines from Campania and its islands which are drunk locally or sent northwards for inclusion in commercial blends.

Further south, into the heel, instep and toe of Italy good wine is even more scarce, although the quaintly named Aglianico del Vulture, a red from Basilicata, on the instep, has a certain reputation outside the area. Its higher quality is due to the altitude – 600 metres or more – at which the vineyards are planted.

SICILY

Sicily, with an island climate, might be expected to do better but, despite the very long history of civilization and viticulture, most of the wines are poorly made, coarse and dull. Marsala, which was made famous through being supplied to Nelson's ships in the 18th century is a fortified, blended and usually sweetened wine with an affinity to Madeira but an underlying bitterness which makes it an acquired taste. Consequently, it is now less frequently exported to countries where it has to compete against the popularity of sherry and port. Its pronounced flavour gives Marsala an important place in cooking and it is used in Zabaglione, a confection made with cream and egg yolks which is a popular sweet throughout Italy. Various similar commercial concoctions are sold already prepared and in bottle.

Corvo is the trade mark of the house of Duca di Salaparuta, a company now owned by the Sicilian regional government, and as a brand is ineligible for DOC status. The quality is achieved by blending of wines from the West and Central areas of the island, some from vineyards at altitudes of over 700 metres. The dry white and full-bodied reds have relatively high acidity giving them life and freshness unusual in a wine from so far south. The sweet dessert wines from Malvasia and Moscato grapes are also attractive.

SARDINIA

Traditionally the wines of Sardinia have been heavy, alcoholic and usually sweet, few concessions being made to tastes outside the island. In recent years the island's economy, one of the most backward in Western Europe, has been given considerable outside aid and, among many new agricultural undertakings, a serious effort is being made to replant vineyards more selectively and provide modern and efficient installations for vinification and handling of the wines. Corsica is already making excellent wine from similar new plantings and Sardinia's turn may soon be coming.

Italian wines are sold with the label of the estate or local Cantine Sociale where they are made or bearing the name of a company, which, like the negoçiants of France, buys the wine, or possibly the grapes, from many different local sources for blending, bottling and ultimate sale. It is wine from the last which is most likely to be found in export markets. There is no easy choice to make between the two, as in Italy small is not necessarily good. Many of the smaller estates under the control of individual proprietors are capable of producing the finest wines in the highest quality areas, but these are mostly snapped up by a faithful private clientele or sold in the great restaurants of the northern Italian cities. Equally, there are many estates, lacking proper equipment for vinification, storage and bottling, which make very mediocre wine indeed. On the other hand, many of the larger co-operatives have been able to afford and install efficient modern plant with a very marked improvement in the standards of wine they make. The large firms, too, have undergone a great deal of expansion in the last decade and are technically as advanced as any in Europe. Inevitably this has been at the expense of individuality but it may be preferable to have a sound, if rather dull, wine than one poorly made and carelessly bottled. Several of the really big companies add to the confusion by spreading their operations across several wine-growing districts and regions.

Spain

ilbao

4 5

Ebro R

Barcelona

E4

6

10

11

7 8 9

E101

17

16

18 Valencia

15

N301

19

17

20

20 21 22

Murcia

N340

7. Priorato
8. Tarragona
9. Penedes
10. Alella
11. Cariñena
12. Mentrida
13. La Mancha
14. Valdepeñas
15. Manchuela
16. Utiel-Requeña

17. Valencia
18. Cheste
19. Almansa
20. Jumilla
21. Yecla
22. Alicante
23. Condado de Huelva
24. Jerez (Sherry)
25. Montilla – Moriles
26. Malaga

1. Ribeiro
2. Valle de Monterrey
3. Valdeorras
4. Rioja
5. Navarra
6. Ampurdan

Spain has more land under vines than any other country in Western Europe, but in terms of production it ranks third after Italy and France. Apart from the mountainous north coast, there is hardly a region which does not make wine of sorts, and there is an enormous variation in style and quality, according to climate, soil and grape varieties, of which there are some hundred. The rainswept hills of Galicia give birth to 'green wines' in the manner of the Portuguese *vinhos verdes;* the temperate north produces the quality growths of the Rioja and Catalonia; the hot central plateau of La Mancha, Extremadura in the west, and the Mediterranean coastal areas of Tarragona and the Levante form a great reservoir of wines for everyday drinking; while Andalusia is the home of aperitif and dessert wines, such as sherry and Málaga.

In all, there are some two dozen demarcated regions, each controlled by its Consejo Regulador or regulating body: Alella, Alicante, Almansa, Ampurdán-Costa Brava, Cariñena, Cheste, Condado de Huelva, Jerez-Xérès-sherry and Manzanilla-Sanlúcar de Barrameda, Jumilla, Málaga, La Mancha, Manchuela, Méntrida, Montilla-Moriles, Navarra, Penedés, Priorato, Ribeiro, Rioja, Tarragona, Utiel-Requena, Valdeorras, Valencia, Valdepeñas and Yecla.

Of an average annual production totalling 32 million hectolitres, the vast demarcated areas of the centre, whose vineyards extend to some 700,000 hectares, make some 9 million hectolitres of wine, most of it in 458 co-operatives supplied by independent growers. Some of this is bottled at source and labelled with the name of the co-operative or private *bodega* (cellar) which made it, but the bulk is sold to *négociants* in Spain or abroad and is often blended and sold under brand names; further large quantities are distilled and used for Spanish brandy.

Classification of wines

In the past, it was the custom to label the mature and better wines, not with the year of vintage, but according to the number of years that they had spent in cask – so that '5° *año*' meant that it had been bottled during the fifth year after the harvest. This is still common practice in Spain itself; but with impending entry into the EEC, labels are falling into line with those from the rest of Europe. They commonly carry the name and type of the wine and that of the *bodega* which made and bottled it; the name of the area in which it was produced; the year of vintage in the form of, say, 'Cosecha 1973'; the degree of alcohol and contents of the bottle; and the stamp or seal of the Consejo Regulador, guaranteeing authenticity and purity. The name of the foreign shipper may also appear; and a back label often incorporates a small map of the demarcated region and the words 'vino con crianza' in the case of a wine matured in cask.

MONTILLA-MORILES

The region of Montilla-Moriles, one of the hottest in Spain, lies in the hills south of Córdoba and produces *flor*-growing wines in the style of sherry.

The vineyards, the best of them around the small towns of Montilla and Moriles, are planted in a sparklingly white and chalky soil resembling the *albariza* of Jerez; they extend to some 18,500 hectares and are mainly farmed by small-holders. The predominant grape is the Pedro Ximénez; but though the region supplies some sweet PX wine to the *bodegas* in Jerez, the grapes here are normally picked earlier and fermented without sunning and to completion, yielding dry wines of from 15·5°-16°·

Montilla differs from sherry in being fermented in large earthenware *tinajas,* but is thereafter matured in identical fashion in a *solera*. Although small amounts of amontillado and oloroso are made, the typical style is an unfortified fino, pale with a greenish tint, and light and very dry on the palate. Average production amounts to some 600,000 hectolitres.

Shippers Alvear, Cobos, Carbonell, Montialbero, and Pérez Barquero.

MÁLAGA

Málaga was an enormously popular 'Ladies' Wine' in Victorian times, but has suffered both from a current lack of interest in sweet dessert wines and from the encroachments of the tourist industry in the Málaga district.

The vineyards, amounting to some 18,000 hectares, lie in the hills to the north and east of the city and belong to small-holders. Of the ten wine varieties approved by the Consejo Regulador the most important are the Lairen, Moscatel, and especially the Pedro Ximénez.

The grapes are either vinified in the mountain villages or brought down to one of the large *bodegas* in Málaga, where all the wine is matured by a modified *solera* system.

The Consejo Regulador lists sixteen types of Málaga, ranging from the very sweet, such as Lágrima Christi and Dulce Color, to a *seco,* or dry wine, and the best have been favourably compared with tawny port. To taste most of these, one must go to Málaga, or at least to Spain, but despite a general decline in production, the best-known of the *bodegas,* Scholtz Hermanos, is fortunately still very much alive and ships its bitter-sweet Solera 1885, one of the best of the Málaga wines.

RIOJA

The Rioja, which makes the best-known Spanish table wines, including red and white in various styles, and rosé, has been famous for its wines since Roman times and before; but they were first made in their present form after the phylloxera epidemic of the late 19th century, when French *vignerons* settled in the region and introduced the methods then current in Bordeaux.

The region lies in northern Spain along the valley of the River Ebro, bounded by hills on either side and extending for some 100 kilometres from the rugged Conchas de Haro in the west to Alfaro near its eastern limit. Logroño, near the centre, stands at 384 metres. It is divided into three sub-regions, the Rioja Alta and Rioja Alavesa to the hillier west, respectively south and north of the Ebro, and the flatter and lower-lying Rioja Baja to the east. The soils vary from calcareous clay in the Rioja Alavesa to a mixture of calcareous and ferruginous clays and alluvial silt in the Rioja Alta, and a predominance of alluvial silt and ferruginous clay in the Rioja Baja.

The vineyards

There are some 46,000 hectares of vineyards in the region as a whole, though with large additions such as the extensive new vineyards of Sogeviña (Pedro Domecq) and Berberana, the area is rapidly growing. A typical traditional *bodega,* La Rioja Alta, owns 130 hectares of vineyard, producing some 30 per cent of its requirement. The balance of fruit is bought from small farmers; apart from those who regularly supply the same *bodega*.

Classification of wines

Red Riojas are bottled either in the round-shouldered claret bottle or in the Burgundy type with sloping shoulders. The claret bottle is used for the lighter wines and the Burgundy type for the fuller-bodied – and also for *all* the red wines from the Rioja Alavesa. White wines are labelled *seco* (dry), *semi-seco* (semi-dry), and *abocado* or *dulce* (sweet).

The name of the *bodega* and its township always appear on the label; but the fact that a *bodega* is located in, say, Haro, does not necessarily mean that its wine is made exclusively with grapes grown in the Rioja Alta, since most of the firms buy a proportion of grapes from the Alavesa. Alavesa wines are almost entirely made with Tempranillo grapes grown in the sub-region.

Blending is so typical of the Rioja that the vintage printed on the label must be taken as meaning that the wine is predominantly of the year stated. *Reservas* are wines aged for six years between cask and bottle.

Grape varieties

Four main varieties of grape are used for making the red wines. The basis is the native Tempranillo, of which the Alavesa wines may contain 90-100 per cent; but those from the Rioja Alta are blended with some 30-40 per cent of Graciano, Mazuelo and Garnacho. The Graciano confers freshness, flavour and aroma; the musts of the Mazuelo are high in tannin, important for wines which are matured for long periods in wood; and the Garnacho, the grape *par excellence* of the Rioja Baja, contributes lightness and alcoholic strength, though its musts oxidize easily, soon turning brick red unless carefully handled. Only two grapes are used for the white wines, the Viura and the Malvasia.

The wines

Like Jerez, the Rioja has individual methods for making wines. The main difference between a Rioja and, say, a Bordeaux or Burgundy is that it is usually aged for much longer in 225-litre *barricas* – hence the typical vanilla-like nose. In the past, the wines were often shipped straight from the barrel without bottle age (which greatly improves them) and it is only fairly recently that the *bodegas* have begun to mature their better wines for a year or two in glass. The regulations of the Consejo Regulador for a minimum period in oak apply equally to white wines. Some, like those of López de Heredia, which may spend seven years in oak, emerge remarkably fresh, but others have been criticized for being maderized and flat. The new tendency is to make white wines *sin crianza* (without ageing) by fermentation below 20°C for periods of up to two months, when they are often deliciously flowery and refreshing.

In general, the red wines from the Rioja Alta are fresher, brisker and longer-lasting than those from the Rioja Alavesa, which are characterized by a softness and gentleness and a very fragrant sweetish nose. The wines from the hotter Rioja Baja, made mainly from the Garnacho, are full-bodied and less delicate, and are often used for blending.

Total production averages 970,000 hectolitres, and some forty of the bodegas have the capacity required by the Consejo Regulador to enable them to export their wines (some of the newer concerns, such as Bodegas Olarra, with its capacity of 30 million litres, are very large indeed).

Vintages

Owing to a more consistent climate, there is not as large a variation between vintages as in Bordeaux or Burgundy, but the best of more recent years were: 1978, 1976, 1975, 1974, 1973, 1970, 1968, 1964 (the best of the century), 1962, 1954.

Shippers In the Rioja Alta: Berberana, Bilbainas, Campo Viejo, Franco Españolas, La Rioja Alta, Lan, Olarra, Marqués de Caceres, Marqués de Murrieta, Montecillo, Muga, López de Heredia, Riojanas and CVNE.
In the Rioja Alavesa: Bodegas Alavesas, Co-operativa de Labastida, Faustino Martínez, Sogeviña (Domecq), Salceda and Marqués de Riscal.

PENEDÉS

Other regions in Catalonia, such as Alella, Priorato and Ampurdán, make wines of repute; but the best-known, rivalling the Riojas, are those from the Penedés. It makes still wines and also sparkling wines by the Champagne method. The Penedés is a small but intensively cultivated region west of Barcelona, extending for some 45 kilometres along the Mediterranean and rising for about the same distance towards the mountains of the interior. The two main centres for winemaking are the small towns of Vilafranca del Penedés and San Sadurní de Noya.

It is a limestone area and is divided into three sub-regions: the hotter Bajo Penedés bordering the coast, particularly suitable for growing grapes for the red wines; the Medio Penedés, where most of the grapes for the sparkling wines are grown; and the higher, cooler and more humid Alto Penedés and San Sadurní de Noya. The latter is hollow with underground cellars and is the headquarters of the large concerns making sparkling wine.

The vineyards

Some of the large firms, such as the Marqués de Monistrol, which makes both still and sparkling wines, and Bodegas Torres, own vineyards extending to some 300 or 400 hectares, but all supplement their grapes with those bought from private farmers; and Codorníu, the largest producer of sparkling wine in the area, owns no vineyards of its own, but buys from some 350 independent growers.

Grape varieties

Native grapes for the red wines are the black Cariñena, Garnacha, Ojo de Liebre (alias the Tempranillo of the Rioja), Samsó and Monastrel. Rosé wines are made with the red Garnacha, and the still whites with the Parellada, a grape which yields wines with a delicately flowery bouquet and full fruity flavour. Sparkling wine is made from the Parellada, Xarel-lo and Macabeo (the Viura of the Rioja).

Apart from these native growths, the forward-looking Bodegas Torres has acclimatized a range of noble vines from abroad. It uses a proportion of Chardonnay for its white Gran Viña Sol; Gewürztraminer and Moscatel for the semi-sweet Esmeralda; Pinot Noir for the red Santa Digna; and Cabernet Sauvignon for the red Gran Coronas wines.

These are not, as in most other parts of Spain, grown low, *a la castellana,* but with stakes and wires; and the white varieties are planted at some 700 metres in the cooler hinterland. The results of this experiment may be judged by the resounding success of the Torres Gran Coronas Black Label at the Gault-Millau 'Olympiad' held in Paris in 1979.

The wines

The still wines from Bodegas Torres are fermented in thermostatically controlled stainless steel tanks, and, unlike the Riojas, the red wines do not spend more than eighteen months to two years in oak casks, with a further period of years in bottle. Torres was also a pioneer in Spain of the growingly popular method of fermenting white wines at low temperature and for prolonged periods, so preserving the aroma and freshness of the fruit.

All the vintages for the white Torres wines from 1970 were good, and apart from 1968 the reds have been good; 1970, 1973 and 1979 were outstanding years.

Apart from Torres, leading producers of still wines are Masia Bach, makers of the luscious and oaky dessert wine, Extrísimo, Bosch-Guell and the Marqués de Monistrol, whose most individual still wine is the refreshing and slightly *pétillant* Vin Natur Blanc de Blanc.

Although the Penedés makes some inexpensive sparkling wine by the *cuve close* process, the great bulk is produced in San Sadurní de Noya by the Champagne method. An interesting innovation, now finding favour in Rheims itself, has been the replacement of the traditional *pupitres* by large hexagonal metal frames, known as *girasols* (or 'sunflowers'), holding some 500 bottles and enabling the throwing of the sediment to be carried out as efficiently and with far less labour.

The underground cellars of Codorníu, extending to nearly 18 kilometres with a storage capacity of 75 million litres, are the largest in the world.

The best of the Penedés sparkling wines, made by the Champagne method, are the extra-dry Brut and Brut Nature, such as the 'Non Plus Ultra' from Codorníu and 'Cordon Negro' and 'Brut Nature' from Freixenet. Among the best recent years were 1969, 1971 and 1973.

Shippers

Still wines: Torres, Masía Bach, Bosch-Guell, Marqués de Monistrol and Mascaró; Sparkling wines: Codorníu, Freixenet, Gonzalez é Dubosc (Jean Perico), Conde de Caralt, Viuda Segura and Castellblanch.

NAVARRA

Bordering the Rioja to the north-east, Navarra makes red, white and rosé wines in rather similar style, though the reds, which account for most of the production perhaps lack something of the intensity and softness of the best Riojas.

The vines are grown in a hilly area between Pamplona to the north and the River Ebro in the south, and the vineyards extend to 22,000 hectares. The Señorío de Sarría grows most of its fruit, the pattern, as elsewhere in Spain, is for the *bodegas* to buy from independent farmers.

Grape varieties

The soils are chalky with deposits of alluvial silt in the river valleys, and, as in the adjacent Rioja Baja, the predominant grape variety is the Garnacho. Smaller quantities of Graciano, Mazuelo and Tempranillo are also used for the red wines, and Sarría uses a little Cabernet Sauvignon and Pinot Noir, introduced to the region from France centuries ago. The white wines are made with Viura and Malvasía; Navarra also produces some sweet Moscatel.

The wines

Average production is about 900,000 hectolitres, the bulk from co-operatives, of which there are eighty-six, and the better wines are vinified and matured by the methods used in the Rioja. The best wines come from the private bodegas.

The excellent Las Campanas red wines from the Vinícola de Navarra are still labelled according to the time spent in cask; the best recent vintages for the Señorío de Sarría were the outstanding 1964, and 1970, 1973, 1975 and 1978.

Shippers Señorio de Sarría, La   Ochoa, and Irrache.
Vinícola de Navarra, Chivite,

VALLADOLID AND LEÓN

Neither of these upland districts, lying respectively to the south-west and west of the Rioja, is demarcated, but Valladolid produces a classic red table wine and some most characterful whites, while the fresh and fruity wines from León have made a promising debut in Britain.

The wines

Vega Sicilia, whose chalky, pine-girt vineyards border the River Duero east of Valladolid at a height of 765 metres, is something of a legend in Spain. Its wines, all of them red, are made in strictly limited quantity from a mixture of the native Tinto Aragonés, Garnacho and white Albillo, and the French Cabernet Sauvignon, acclimatized after the vineyards were affected by phylloxera. Vinified and matured in oak in traditional fashion, they spend years in cask acquiring a deep bouquet and fruity flavour.

Vega Sicilia is never sold less than ten years old, and the wine currently available is the 1966. Valbuena, made from the same grapes and by the same methods, is labelled either as '3-year-old' or '5-year-old'.

Rueda, the other side of Valladolid to the west, makes *flor*-growing white wines, high in alcohol and with a sherry-like flavour.

The traditional wines from León, lying at about the same height as the Rioja and to the west, were red heavyweights, peasant-made or produced in the co-operatives. Largely thanks to the establishment by the main wholesalers of a winery equipped with the most modern plant, Planta de Elaboración y Embotellado de Vinos S.A., the region is now making and shipping a range of fresh and fruity wines, red, rosé and white, some with long ageing in oak.

Non-vintage wines, such as the red and white Rey León from V.I.L.E. are excellent value for money, but the reds improve after a few years in oak. There are also seventeen co-operatives in León.

Producers Vega Sicilia near Valladolid, the Co-operativa Ribera de Duero in Peñafiel, and V.I.L.E. and Valdeobispo in the León district. The Marqués de Riscal makes its white wine with grapes grown near Rueda.

Shippers in Valladolid, Vega Sicilia and the Co-operativa Ribera de Duero; in León, V.I.L.E. and Valdeobispo.

GALICIA

In its wines, as in other matters, Galicia, in the west and mountainous far north-west of Spain, is a region apart. Its most typical wines are *pétillant* in the manner of the *vinhos verdes* from the adjacent region of Portugal across the Minho river, and are often made with same grapes.

The soils are mainly granitic, and with few exceptions the vineyards – large in extent but small in size, of which only 8,000 hectares are demarcated – are cultivated by peasant farmers.

Around Valdeorras, Monterrey and Verín, towards the east, the vines are grown low and produce still wines; elsewhere, the high-growing tree vine predominates. Of the dozens of grape varieties, the best is the white Albariño, used to make a *pétillant* wine undergoing malo-lactic fermentation.

Producers The co-operatives of Verín, Monterrey, Valdeorras, Ribadavia, and the *bodega* of the Marqués de Figueroa at Fefiñanes, which makes a very superior Albariño wine.

The only Galician wines shipped to the UK are the still white and red from the co-operative at Valdeorras.

Wines in bulk

Seas of sound wine for everyday drinking, mostly made in the hundreds of co-operatives, are produced in the vast demarcated areas of the centre and Levante: Mancha, Méntrida, and Almansa – 6,150,000 hectolitres; Valdepeñas – 620,000 hectolitres; Utiel-Requena, Valencia and Cheste – 965,000 hectolitres; and Alicante, Yecla and Jumilla – 890,000 hectolitres. The more charicterful growths are:

Valpedeñas This town, with bodegas in every street, has long been famous for its strong but often surprisingly fresh red wines, made in great earthenware *tinajas* from the Cencibel, Monastrel and Tintorera grapes.

Utiel-Requena Lying west of Valencia on high ground bordering the great central plateau, its wines are light, well-balanced *claretes* from the black Bobal.

Yecla and **Jumilla** The problem in these regions, further south in the hills behind Alicante, is that the prolonged summer heat leads to excessive amounts of sugar in the grapes and wines that are overstrong in alcohol. It is being tackled by earlier picking and fermentation in closed vats; and the lighter and much improved Spanish-bottled growths in these areas augur well for the future.

Shippers In Valdepeñas, Bodegas Morenito; in Utiel-Requena, Casa de Calderón; in Valencia, the huge Vinival, a consortium of the old-established firms of Mompó, Teschendorff and Steiner; in Yecla, Co-operativa la Purísima; in Jumilla, Co-operativa San Isidro; and in La Mancha, Co-operativa La Daimileleña.

SHERRY

Sherry has had many imitators, but remains unique among aperitif and dessert wines.

As early as the fourteenth century, Chaucer commented on the strength and 'fumositee' of the wines from nearby Lepe; but it was after the expulsion of the Jews from Spain in 1492 that British and other foreign wine merchants moved into the region in strength. At that time the wine was known as 'sack' (probably from the Spanish *sacar*, to 'export'), hence Falstaff's famous complaint, "O monstrous! but one halfpenny worth of bread to this intolerable deal of sack".

Its popularity in England was secured by Drake's raid on Cádiz in 1587 and his seizure of nearly 3,000 casks of wine. After a temporary decline in popularity during the earlier part of the eighteenth century, attributable to the Methuen Treaty of 1703, which gave preference to Portuguese wines, the trade with England picked up during the last decades of the century. There was a tremendous expansion after the Peninsular War during the early 1800's and it was from this era onwards that the great sherry houses of today took shape. In the wake of the War, British merchants, such as the Scot, C P Gordon who later became British Vice-Consul in Jerez, played a major role in reviving the trade.

The amalgamation of British and Spanish interests, reinforced by intermarriage between the great sherry dynasties, is typical of the history of the trade. The memory of many English, Scots and Irish merchants is enshrined in the household names of today: Duff Gordon, Osborne, Garvey, Gonzalez Byass, Harveys, Sandeman, William and Humbert. The famous British sherry house, Harveys, market the biggest selling of all sherry – Harveys Bristol Cream – which is sold in no less than one hundred countries. The Bristol firm owns one of the largest bodega sites in the centre of Jerez and Harveys also jointly possess over 2,000 acres of vineyards making them one of the biggest vineyard owners in the area.

The British influence is still strong in Jerez which is not surprising as although a Spanish product, sherry has been developed over the centuries to British taste and much of the mystique which surrounds it is now British. Britain imports almost half of all sherry shipments from Spain and the British have been responsible for spreading the popularity of this Spanish wine throughout the world.

The Jerez district is fan-shaped, lying between the Gualdalquivir and Guadalete Rivers and the Atlantic, and including the town of Sanlúcar de Barrameda, Jerez de la Frontera and Puerto de Sta. Maria. The vineyards lie to the north and west of the town of Jerez up to Sanlúcar de Barrameda on the Guadalquivir River and beyond Chiclana de la Frontera – south of Puerto de Sta. Maria and Cádiz.

The vineyards

In all, the vineyards extend to 22,250 ha and are planted on a series of rolling hills. The best of the soils, though least prolific in terms of yield, is the *albariza,* a dazzling white in summer and containing some 40 per cent of chalk, the residue consisting of clay and sand. It is able to absorb and to hold large amounts of water without caking, a most important attribute in a region where the average rainfall amounts to only 22 inches and temperatures rise to 40°C for most of the summer. Other types of soil, used for grapes yielding the sweeter and heavier wines, are a dark mud clay, *barro,* and the sandy *arena,* both containing some ten per cent of chalk.

Among the vineyards you may occasionally still see the *bienteveos,* rough shelters made of poles roofed with esparto grass and formerly manned by armed guards, who would shoot on sight thieves helping themselves to the ripe grapes. There is, indeed, a proverb in Jerez:

Las niñas y las viñas difíciles son de guardar
(Girls and vineyards are difficult to guard)

Grape varieties

Of the many types of grape once grown in the area, only three are now of major importance. The Palomino blanco,

grown in the *albariza* soil is the sherry grape *par excellence* and is largely used for making *finos* and *amontillados*. Smaller amounts of Pedro Ximénez and Moscatel are grown for blending to make sweet wines, and for this purpose the grapes are left out in the sun on grass mats to concentrate the sugar content. There is a legend about the Pedro Ximenez to the effect that it originated in the Canaries, was thence taken to the Rhine and brought to Jerez by a soldier of the Emperor Charles V, one Peter Siemens, in the seventeenth century; unfortunately the story is probably more colourful than true! In the past, the grapes were crushed in wooden troughs by labourers wearing *zapatos de pisar,* cowhide boots studded with flat tacks, but this picturesque ceremony has now been abandoned in favour of horizontal presses, first devised in Germany, which work by squeezing the grapes against the side of a stainless steel cylinder by means of an inflatable rubber bag – so avoiding the rupture of skins and pips. Fermentation, formerly carried out in oak butts, nowadays takes place in stainless steel tanks. Thereafter, sherry is treated in a way unlike any other wine, the *must* (as it is referred to for the first few years) being left to stand in loosely-stoppered oak butts. With other wines, this would normally result in oxidation and the eventual conversion of the wine to vinegar, but in Jerez a film of yeasts, known as the *flor,* soon develops on the surface of the liquid, so regulating the access of air. As the wine grows older, and also stronger in alcohol because of loss of water vapour through the pores of the oak, the *flor* becomes thinner, sinking to the bottom of the barrel. After a year or two, during which it has been racked and sparingly fortified, the wine is classified according to type and character. The lighter, more delicate wines are set aside for *finos* and *amontillados;* and the fuller-bodied with little or no *flor,* destined for *olorosos,* are further fortified to kill the yeast.

Another characteristic of sherry is that it is matured in a *solera,* consisting of long rows of butts, known as 'scales' containing wine of similar type, but progressively younger in age. The number of scales varies according to the type of sherry, but is usually not less than five – it is incidentally a common, but mistaken belief that the casks at the top contain the youngest wine and those lower down the older. The different scales may not in fact all be housed in the same building. When wine is required for shipment or bottling, it is drawn off from the butts first laid down, which are then 'refreshed' with rather less mature wine, and so on down all the 'scales' to the youngest wine in the *criadera* (or 'nursery'). This is called 'working the scales' and the process is practicable because the younger wine rapidly takes on the character of the older and results in a uniform end product from year to year. The operation of the solera is entrusted to the *capataz* or cellarman, whose chosen instrument for sampling and checking the wine is the long-handled venencia, with a silver cup at one end, plunged into the butt through the bung-hole and designed to avoid undue disturbance of the *flor*.

Classification of sherry

Finos Pale straw-coloured, light and very dry, containing some 15-16° of alcohol, and the most delicate and refreshing of sherries. They are at their best when freshly bottled; once a bottle has been opened it should be consumed within a few days, and the wine should be drunk chilled.

Manzanilla A pale, crisp and very dry *fino* with the salty tang of the sea air from Sanlúcar de Barrameda, where it is made in *soleras* sometimes containing as many as 14 'scales'.

Amontillados Made by further maturation of *finos* in cask, are amber yellow in colour with a dry, nutty flavour and of about 16·5-18° strength. Cheaper *amontillados* are not always made in this way, but are blends approximating the flavour and style.

Olorosos Bone dry in their natural state, dark in colour, fuller-bodied and soft, these are the most fragrant of sherries and may approach 24° when old.

Cream sherries Were originally developed for the British market, but have become increasingly popular in other countries, particularly in the USA. They are of two types. The dark, mahogany-coloured variety is made by sweetening an *oloroso* with a sweet must made from Pedro Zimenez (and other grapes) left to dry in the sun. The base wine for *pale creams* is a *fino*, sweetened with *dulce apagado*, a wine made by checking the final stages of fermentation with brandy, so leaving some of the grape sugar.

Amorosos A traditional name for a smooth, sweet oloroso (from the Spanish word meaning 'loving'), now usually referred to as cream sherry. Unlike *finos*, sweetened *olorosos* of good quality improve in bottle, ending up with a finish that is bitter-sweet or even dry.

Palo Cortado It is extremely difficult to operate a *solera* for this type of sherry, at its best a superb wine, somewhat between an *oloroso* and *amontillado* in style.

Shippers

In Jerez de la Frontera, Croft, Pedro Domecq, Garvey, Gonzalez Byass, John Harvey and Sons, Bodegas Internacionales, Lustau, Sandeman, Zoilo Ruiz-Mateos, Valdespino and Williams & Humbert; in Puerto de Sta. Maria, Duff Gordon, Osborne, Terry; and in Sanlucar de Barrameda, Antonio Barbadillo.

Portugal

Like Spain with her sherry, Portugal is best-known for a single wine, port; and by far her largest exports of wine are of the sparkling rosés, such as Mateus. But Portugal makes a variety of good table wines, which are belatedly receiving attention abroad thanks to their outstanding value.

With only a fifth of the land area of Spain, Portugal produces a third as much wine, most of it from the area north of Lisbon and the Tagus, where the land rises progressively from a narrow coastal strip to the high sierras of the Spanish border. Although some of the port firms and a few other large concerns own extensive vineyards of their own, northern Portugal is a land of small farmers, and some 15 per cent of the population earns its living by making or selling wine.

Only three of the demarcated regions, Douro (port), Vinhos Verdes and Dão, are of any size, and though the remaining four near Lisbon – Colares, Carcavelos, Bucelas, and Moscatel de Setúbal – produce excellent wine, their production is miniscule. There are now plans afoot for demarcating other regions producing much larger amounts of table wine, such as Bairrada, the Upper Douro and Ribatejo.

Classification of wines

Of the average annual production of 10 million hectolitres of wine, exports in 1977 totalled 1,314,967 hectolitres of table wine and 485,950 hectolitres of port. Most of this is bottled and labelled in Portugal, rather than being shipped in bulk.

Wines from the demarcated areas are labelled with the name of the producer and region, the contents and degree of alcohol, and the vintage. *Vinhos verdes* carry no vintage year because they are always bottled and shipped in the spring following the harvest, and drunk young. The Selo de Origem, or guarantee of the official regulating body, appears, not on the label, but in the form of a narrow, numbered paper strip affixed to the cork and neck of the bottle before capsuling.

The labelling of wines from undemarcated regions varies a good deal. They may carry all the above information (without, of course, the Selo de Origem), but a wine such as the well-made Serradayres from the Ribatejo bears nothing except the name of the shipper, the year of vintage and a list, now frowned on by the EEC, of prizes won in the past.

VINHOS VERDES

The *vinhos verdes,* or 'green wines', which are low in alcohol (9° to 11.5°), slightly *pétillant,* and light and fresh, are among

1 Vinho Verde
2 Douro
3 Dão
4 Colares
5 Bucelas
6 Carcavelos
7 Moscatel de Setúbal

ADEGA COOPERATIVA DE PONTE DO LIMA

0.75 L.

VINHO VERDE

REGIÃO DEMARCADA

BRANCO

ENGARRAFADO NA ORIGEM

Portugal's most individual. The area is bound by the Minho river to the north, the Atlantic to the west and the port country to the east, and extends a little south of Oporto. The soils are granitic, and the relatively high rainfall has led to the training of the vines up trees, on trellises, or on wires strung between *cruzetas,* well clear of the ground.

It is an intensively cultivated area, and the 24,972 hectares of vineyards are, in the main, cultivated by some 95,000 small-holders, most of whom take their grapes to be vinified in one of the twenty-one cooperatives supervised by the official Comissão de Viticultura da Região dos Vinhos Verdes.

The making of the wine is again entirely individual and turns on the elimination of the harsh-tasting malic acid present in large amount in the grapes, during a so-called malo-lactic fermentation which follows the first fermentation. Malic acid is converted to the smoother lactic, and the introduction of carbon dioxide accounts for the *pétillance* – though it is usual to add a little gas artificially. The wines are ready for drinking in the late spring after the harvest, and in their natural state are bone dry; some are now sweetened a little for foreign consumption.

The wines

The region's production is divided into 70 per cent of a some-what brusque red wine which is not exported much, as against only 30 per cent of the delicate white known abroad. White grapes include the Azal, Pederña and Trajadura, but the best are the Loureiro, grown in most of the six sub-regions – Monção, Basto, Amarante, Braga, Penafiel and Lima – and the Alvarinho, grown only in Monção.

Vinhos Verdes should be drunk while fresh and young, stored in cool surroundings and chilled in the refrigerator before opening. The fruitiest, most delicate and fragrant wines, such as the Palacio de Brejoeira, made with the Alvarinho grape, and the Quinta de San Claudio made from the Loureiro, are estate-bottled and obtainable only in Portugal.

Producers Apart from superior estate-made wines, such as those from the Quinta de San Claudio, the Palacio de Brejoeira and Aveleda, most originate from the co-operatives and are blended and bottled by such firms as Casalinho, Borges and Irmão, Ribalonga, Barbosa, Aliança, and Monteiro. Additionally, a large consortium of co-operatives, Vercoope, blends and ships direct.

109

DÃO,

The Dão, which produces some of the best of Portugal's table wines, 90 per cent of them red, is an upland area in the north-east, lying between the Serra da Estrela and the Caramulo mountains and centring on the old Moorish town of Viseu. The demarcated area extends to 376,400 hectares, of which only a twentieth or about 18,000 hectares, is under vines.

The Dão is splashed with pine trees and outcrops of granite, and some of the soil is so hard that it has to be blasted and broken up with crowbars before planting. Ninety per cent of the grapes are grown in the tiny vineyards of some 40,000 smallholders. The main grape varieties are: for the red wines, Touriga Nacional, Tinta Pinheira, Alverelhão, Bastardo, and Jaen; and for the whites, Arinto, Barcelo and Verdelho. There are few sizeable private *adegas* – though that of the Conde de Santar is one – and the vast bulk of the grapes are vinified in one of the ten co-operatives operated by the Federação dos Vinicultores de Dão. A characteristic of the wines is the high glycerine content, resulting from continued slow fermentation during the winter.

The wines

Red Dãos tend to be somewhat tannic when young. They should be opened an hour or two before serving. The small extra expense of a *reserva* or *garrafeira* (a wine with prolonged bottle-age and a plain white label) is always worthwhile. Owing to the widespread habit of blending, it is difficult to pick out vintages, but 1970 was perhaps the best of the last decade. The white wines have been criticized for being too oaky and somewhat flat and maderized, but some of the 1977s and 1978s – the Grão Vasco, for example – are clean and refreshing.

The Dão produces an annual average of 500,000 hectolitres of wine, most of which is bought by large private firms who blend and mature it in oak, either in *adegas* in the region or in Oporto and elsewhere, and ship under their own labels.

Shippers Vinícola do Vale do Dão (Grão Vasco), J. M. da Fonseca (Terras Altas), Aliança, Casalinho, Caves Velhas, Borges and Irmão, Barbosa, and the Real Vinícola do Norte de Portugal. The Conde de Santar makes a superior estate-grown wine, shipped by Carvalho, Ribeiro and Ferreira.

DEMARCATED WINES OF THE CENTRE

Two of these tiny regions, Carcavelos and Colares, are threatened by urban encroachment from Lisbon. The red wines from Colares, tannic when young but beautiful when aged in oak, are of great historic interest, since the vines grown in dune sands and were not affected by phylloxera. Bucelas makes dry and elegant white wine from the Arinto grape. The Moscatel de Setúbal, from the Arrábida peninsula, just south of Lisbon and the Tagus, is one of the world's great dessert wines and is shipped as '6-year-old' or '25-year-old'.

Producers

Colares, Adega Regional de Colares; Carcavelos, Quinta do Barão; Bucelas, João Camile

Alves and Caves Velhas: Moscatel de Setúbal, J.M. da Fonseca.

Sparkling Rosés

The rosés, produced in various regions of Portugal in huge modern complexes from a variety of red grapes, are lightly aerated by pumping in carbon dioxide under pressure. They account for 80 per cent of the country's wine exports; between them, the two leading producers, SOGRAPE (makers of Mateus) and J.M. da Fonseca (with its Lancers), ship some 2 million cases a year to the United States alone.

Mateus and Lancers are household words, but sparkling rosés are also made by other large companies, including Caves Dom Teodosio, Caves Império, Real Companhía Vinícola and Aliança.

UNDEMARCATED WINES

It has long been apparent that Portugal stands in need of the radical new demarcation now under way. A vast amount of table wine, often more than drinkable, is made in the Ribatejo just north of Lisbon, Bairrada to the south of Oporto, and in the Upper Douro valley (at present demarcated only for port). There are other smaller enclaves, such as Buçaco on the fringe of the Dão, Pinhel and Borba near the Spanish frontier, Gaieras near Óbidos, and Palmela in the Arrábida peninsula, which produce wines, mainly red, some of which are first-rate – not to mention the marvellous red Ferreirinha, made by the port firm of Ferreira. The Algarve, so popular with summer visitors, also makes wine around Lagoa: this is pleasant enough for holiday drinking, but is undistinguished.

Of the other undemarcated wines, space prevents mention of all but a very few, all red: Serradayres (Carvalho, Ribeiro and Ferreira) from the Ribatejo; Evel (Real C. a Vinícola) and Vila Real tinto (SOGRAPE) from the Upper Douro: Barracão (Caves do Barrocão) from the Bairrada; Periquita and Camarate (J.M. da Fonseca) from Setúbal; the very superior Buçaco wines, obtainable only on the spot at the Palace Hotel; and the superb Barca Velha (Ferreira) from the Douro.

PORT

Portugal is England's oldest ally, and her wines have been shipped since the twelfth century. There had been a change in emphasis of trading patterns by the late 1600s, when the British were exporting wool and salt cod – the *bacalhau* still so popular in Portugal – in exchange for colonial products from Brazil. When the spices and sugar from the New World began reaching England direct, it became necessary to find an alternative trading commodity; and it was at this time that the wines from the Douro valley were first shipped.

Unfortunately they were rough in comparison with the French wines, to which the British were accustomed, and inspired popular jingles, such as:

Mark how it smells. Methinks, a real pain
Is by its odour thrown upon my brain...

However, with Britain and France moving towards open war over the issue of the Spanish Succession, the government in London was determined to discourage the traditional trade in claret, and the famous Methuen Treaty was signed in 1703, giving preference to Portuguese wines.

Resolute efforts were now made to improve the quality of the product from the Douro. The problem was that the grapes, rich in sugar, were fermented to fast and furious completion in open stone troughs (or *lagars*), losing much of

DOURO VALLEY

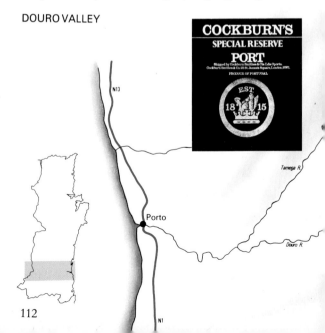

their flavour and aroma and all of the residual sugar in the process. About 1720 the growers hit upon the device of adding brandy to the must during the last stages of fermentation, so killing the yeasts and leaving a little sugar in the wine. This is in effect how port has been made ever since; but, in the words of a contemporary, the first samples with the spirit incompletely amalgamated, burnt 'like fire in the stomach'. In a concerted effort to improve the wines, the British merchants, large numbers of whom had settled in Oporto, founded the Association of Port Wine Shippers, later building the Factory House as their headquarters.

The Portuguese government now took a hand, and in 1765 a leading statesman, the forceful Marquis of Pombal, founded the Port Wine Company, which established new standards of quality, forbidding practices such as the flavouring and colouring of the wine with elderberries and demarcating the wine-growing area.

In 1833, by which time the Company itself had fallen a victim to abuse, the monopoly was dissolved and port was well on the way to being the wine we know today. Much of the credit for perfecting it must go to a devoted British merchant, J.J. Forrester – another enemy of the ill-famed elderberry – who arrived from England in 1831 to join his uncle's firm of Webber, Forrester and Cramp (now Offley, Forrester). He

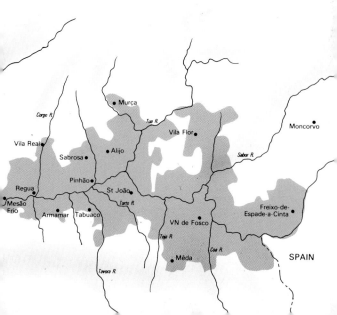

was later created a Baron by the Portuguese government in recognition of his services and died tragically in 1862, when the boat in which he was returning to Oporto from the vineyards capsized and sank in the rapids of the River Douro. The oldest of the port firms, that of C.N. Kopke & Co Ltd was founded in 1638 by Christian Kopke, the first Consul General for the Hanseatic Free Towns. Ferreira, the biggest of the Portuguese-owned concerns, dates from 1751, but owes its early success to Donna Antonia Adelaide Ferreira, born in 1810, whose firm and characterful face, in blue tiles, looks down on visitors today at the company's great Lodge in Vila Nova de Gaia. It was her husband who founded the Quinta do Vesúvio, the largest estate in the Upper Douro, and planted hundreds of thousands of vines covering seven hills and thirty valleys.

The oldest established English firm is Warre & Co. which began trading as John Clark in 1670, followed by Croft and Co, founded as Phayre and Bradley in 1678 and Quarles Harris in 1680. With the stimulus of the Methuen Treaty, others followed thick and fast: Offley, Forrester (1729), Hunt Roope (1735), Sandeman (1790), Graham (1814) and Cockburn's (1815), which is now the biggest port shipper in Britain.

The British influence in Oporto remains even stronger than in Jerez, the sherry centre of Spain. The sons of the port community usually go to English schools and marry English girls. There is a cricket club with regular fixtures; and the most obvious symbol of 'Britishness' is the Factory House, now a club for the senior partners of the Association of the 13 British port shippers. Among its many amenities are complete files of *The Times,* dating from the first issue, and twin dining rooms, into the second of which the members retreat at the end of a meal so as to enjoy their port free from the odours of food.

The Vineyards

The port region extends from just west of Regua, a railhead for the despatch of the wine to the Lodges in Oporto, to the Spanish frontier in the east. The wild and mountainous Douro valley, with its blistering summers and winter rains, is difficult country for vines. They are grown on narrow terraces blasted into the hillsides, held by retaining walls and connected by narrow stairways. Some have been abandoned because of the high cost of labour.

The soil is a hard pre-Cambrian schist, rich in potassium, but containing very little nitrate, phosphate, calcium or organic material. Of some twenty varieties of grape used for making the red wines, the best is the Touriga Nacional, resembling the Cabernet Sauvignon. Other well-known varieties are the Souzão. Mourisco Semente, Tinta Francisca, Bastardo and Alvarelhão. The main white grapes are the Dona Branca, Códega, Gauveio, and varieties of Malvasia and Moscatel.

A large proportion of the grapes is bought from the numerous small farmers, some of whom also make wine in their *quintas,* but all the famous port firms own their own vineyards too.

The grapes are vinified in the Upper Douro and were traditionally pressed barefoot in square granite *lagars,* the ceremony continuing long into the night by the light of hurricane lamps and to the accompaniment of concertinas, guitars, fiddles and drums. Nowadays at the *quintas* of the large shippers it is more common to use mechanical crushers and to ferment the must in modern closed vinification vats, originally used in Algeria and working on the coffee percolator principle. Once the sugar content has fallen to between 8.5-6° baumé, further fermentation is checked by adding grape spirit, so killing the yeasts and preserving the natural grape sugar, the residual sweetness which is typical of the wine.

In an average year, some 200,000 pipes (of 534 litres) are made but of these only 90,000 emerge as port. A points system, which takes into consideration the characteristics of the vineyard, the form of cultivation and the grape variety and, most important, the yield from the grapes (a *low* yield is preferable), is used to assess the suitability of the new wine for further elaboration. It is then left until the spring, when it is transported to the Shippers' Lodges in Vila Nova de Gaia, across the river from Oporto. For centuries, the wine was ferried down the rapids of the Douro in the high-prowed *barcos rabelos,* with their single square sail; these gave way to trains, once a railway had been constructed to Regua and Pinhao; but most of the wine is now transported in tanker lorries.

Rambling, old-fashioned buildings with red-tiled roofs, the Lodges themselves, crowded along the granite quays of the Douro, retain their traditional character. Cement *depositos* are used for temporary storage; but blending and maturing are carried out, first in large vats and later in oak pipes of 534 litres, for the finer wines and of chestnut for the others.

Port is aged and blended according to style, and the different types are:

Vintage Port The aristocrat of the wines, made exclusively from grapes harvested in a single particularly good year. *Lotes* or parcels of different wine of the same vintage are first aged in oak pipes for about two years, after which they are blended and bottled. England has always been the largest market for vintage port and it was formerly shipped in cask and bottled by the importer, but since the last War bottling has increasingly been carried out at the Lodges. Vintage port throws a heavy crust and must be decanted.

Crusted or Crusting Port A blend of *lotes* from different vintages, aged rather longer in wood, hence maturing more quickly, but still spending a prolonged period in bottle and so throwing a crust. It has not quite the same balance as vintage port and is shorter-lived and ready to drink in five to eight years.

Tawny Port A blended wine, aged for several years in cask. Lighter in colour, smooth and less full-bodied, fine tawny port has been described as 'the port man's port'. The genuine article is by no means cheap, and the name has been much abused, since there are 'tawny ports' on the market which owe their pale colour to blending with cheaper, light-coloured wines, or even with white port.

Late Bottled Vintage Port Resembles vintage port only in consisting of wine entirely from the same year, but spends a longer period, up to five years, in wood. It does not throw a crust and develops an entirely individual flavour and vintage bouquet but has sometimes unfairly come into disrepute for being sold in restaurants as vintage port or because blends of ruby have been passed off in its name.

Ruby Is a blend of relatively young wines matured in wood. Good ruby port is, however, by no means to be despised or relegated to cooking and when kept in bottle for a few years may greatly improve.

All of the above types of wine are made from black grapes but there are also *white ports* always matured in wood, and traditionally sweet or very sweet. This style of wine is inordinately popular in France as a pre-dinner aperitif and has helped to account for the boom in sales to the Continent which, in terms of bulk, now buys more port than Britain. Although still called the Englishman's wine, the French have for some time drunk far more port than the British, currently accounting for 38% of all port consumption. Britain follows with 12% and the remaining leading world port markets, all Europe, are Portugal, Belgium and Luxembourg, Italy, Netherlands, West Germany and Denmark. More recently, the shippers have introduced dry white ports, made by fermenting out the grapes before fortifying the wine. Though the best of them are round and fruity, none are as dry as *fino* sherry and lack its distinctive, fresh crispness.

Quality control is very strict. The port firms must submit samples of all their wines to the Instituto do Vinho do Porto, where they undergo some thirty stringent laboratory tests. Thereafter, the wines are tasted by a panel of master tasters. If a wine is rejected and the shipper appeals, it is submitted to a further blind tasting with others, against which no appeal is possible; if the wine does not meet the standards of the panel, an order is made for its conversion to brandy.

Shippers A.A. Calem & Co., Cockburn Smithes & Co., Croft & Co., Delaforce Sons & Co., Dow & Co., A.A. Ferreira, Feuerheerd Bros & Co., Fonseca, W.J. Graham & Co., Guimaraens Vinhos S.A.R.L., Gonzalez Byass & Co., C.N. Kopke & Co., Mackenzie, Driscoll & Co., Martinez Gassiot & Co. Ltd., Morgan Bros., Offley Forrester Ltd., Quarles Harris & Co., Sandeman, George G. & Co. Ltd., A.J. Da Silva & Co., Smith Woodhouse & Co., Taylor Fladgate & Yeatman and Warre & Co.

MADEIRA

The other great Portuguese dessert and aperitif wine is Madeira, made on the island in the Atlantic. The best of the growths are from the south and are cultivated by small-holders in their mountain plots, in a soil consisting of a mixture of clay and volcanic cinder.

Types of Madeira

Madeira is labelled by the grapes used to make it which, in increasing order of sweetness, are Sercial, Verdelho, Bual, and Malmsey. Good Madeira is not cheap, but the maturer wines repay the money spent on them.

Sercial The driest of the wines, it is fermented out to consume most of the sugar and is best drunk as an aperitif or with soup.
Verdelho A sweeter wine, but may still be drunk as an aperitif – or, of course, with a slice of Madeira cake.

Bual and **Malmsey.** Made by adding brandy to check fermentation, these are sweet, full-bodied dessert wines.

Production

Madeira is unique in being 'stoved' (heated up) for some months at between 45°C to 50°C, a process introduced after it was found that the passage of the wine through the tropics in sailing ships much improved the quality. It is then fortified and matured in cask for a minimum of three years. This wine benefits more than any other from prolonged ageing in the bottle.

Producers Average annual production is 140,000 hectolitres, and leading producers are: Blandy's, Cossart Gordon, Ferraz, Henriques and Henriques, Leacock, Lomelino, Sandeman, and Shortridge Lawton.

United States of America

The history of winemaking

The history of grape-growing and winemaking in the
United States stems from many roots. One can dip back to
about the 11th century when the intrepid Norwegian explorer, Leif Erickson, was reputed to have stepped off his
boat, somewhere along the north-eastern coast of the country. Finding his way inland hindered by a tangle of vines and
heavy undergrowth, the Norse rover decided to call this new
discovery Vineland.

But if Erickson's account is dismissed as just so much
romance, the grapevine's introduction into America starts
with the Colonists who settled in the 1500s along the eastern
coastline. These hardy souls suffered many hardships, not to
mention the fact that their favourite wines, made from Old
World varieties of Vitis vinifera, were unavailable in the
New World. So they reluctantly made wine from the native
North American grapes of the species Vitis labrusca, riparia
and rotundifolia. A variety named Scuppernong from the
rotundifolia grape family was, perhaps, the first American
vine.

Legend has it that Sir Walter Raleigh first discovered the
Scuppernong in about 1526 on Roanoke Island, off Virginia.
Today, the 'Mother Vine', a 300-year-old supervine with a
trunk over half a metre (2 feet) thick is still a major tourist
attraction on the island.

While the new nation was slowly moving westward, car-
rying the native vines along, Franciscan priests were trek-
king northward from Mexico into New Mexico and Alta
California (now Southern California). They brought with
them a Spanish grape called Criolla to produce the altar wines
for a string of missions that were going up along the coast all
the way north to Sonoma. Criolla – or the Mission grape, as
it was soon to be known – became the base for the Californian
wine industry, and continues to be cultivated today in over
1600 hectares (4000 acres).

Colonists soon tired of the intense, musky, 'foxy' flavour of
the native grapes though, and sent back to Europe for
familiar vines which would yield a wine more to their liking.
Thus began a struggle to coax these more delicate, disease-
prone vines to grow in the harsh climate of the east. Eventually, the Mission gave way to more sophisticated varieties,
thanks mainly to pioneers like the Hungarian emigré, Agoston Haraszthy.

Grape-growing was on the increase, with states like Ohio,
New York, Pennsylvania, and Virginia, fast becoming ma-

jor regions of wine production. For more than 150 years (1619–1773), Vinifera grapes were grown successfully by such noted Americans as Thomas Jefferson in Virginia, William Penn in Pennsylvania and Lord Delaware in Maryland.

Like many other undertakings in this huge land, winemaking grew fast in certain, almost isolated regions. While the Eastern states were discovering the Labrusca, California winemakers were cultivating Viniferas. By 1857, Haraszthy had made his trip to Europe, returning with thousands of vines and cuttings.

It was National Prohibition, which became law in 1920, that was the major downfall for many American wineries. Despite the restrictions imposed, some continued to make altar wines and other non-wine drinks and mixes, until repeal thirteen years later.

Today, California produces over 70 per cent of the nation's wine and continues to lead the country in innovative and expansive improvements in viticulture and enology. New York, experimenting more every year with hybrids and vinifera, is second to California, but the gap in production nearly matches the 5000-kilometre (3000-mile) distance between the two states.

Production

In 1979, the United States produced 13·4 million hectolitres (352·4 million gallons) of wine, an increase of just over 600,000 hectolitres (15 million gallons) made in 1978. Of the 1979 total, 9·25 million hectolitres (243·6 million gallons) were in table wines, 850,000 hectolitres (22·3 million gallons) in sparkling wines and the remainder in dessert wines. Only table and sparkling wines have been showing an increase in recent years. California, with 71 per cent of the nation's total, produced 11·8 million hectolitres (314·2 million gallons), while all other states provided 1·5 million hectolitres (38·7 million gallons) of wine.

CALIFORNIA
History and development

Various pioneer settlers have been credited with the beginning of California's wine history. The most likely candidate was the Spanish explorer, Cortez, who moved into the new world in about 1524, planting vineyards along the way, though historians are not sure which grapes he brought with him from the Old World.

Vineyard expansion moved slowly until the late 1700s when Franciscan priests introduced the Criolla grape into California and New Mexico. The padres had designs on a new trail

OREGON

CALIFORNIA

Klamath R.

Trinity R.

Shasta Lake

Pitt R.

Eel R.

NEVADA

5

Sacramento R.

80

Ukiah

Clear Lake

Russian R.

St. Helena

Tahoe Lake

Santa Rosa

American R.

Napa

Sacramento

Lodi

San Francisco

Oakland

Stockton

Modesto

San Jose

Owens R.

Salinas

Fresno

San Joaquin R.

Monterey

Salinas R.

5

Kern R.

ESTATE BOTTLED

S. Luis Obispo

Bakersfield

Geyser Peak

Irrigation Canal

1979 SONOMA COUNTY

FUMÉ BLANC
(DRY SAUVIGNON BLANC)

Santa Barbara

Los Angeles

PRODUCED & BOTTLED BY GEYSER PEAK WINERY, GEYSERVILLE,
SONOMA COUNTY, CALIFORNIA   ALCOHOL 12% BY VOLUME.

120

of missions up and down the wilds of the western continent and altar wines would be needed to celebrate mass.

In 1767, Father Junípero Serra journeyed north from Baja California to found the Mission San Diego. Padre Serra brought with him more Criolla which he succeeded in planting in more than twenty-one missions along the Camino Real or King's Highway. By 1824, the mission trail had stretched from San Diego, northward to Sonoma. Settlers who built their new lives around the missions began to grow Criolla (eventually to be called Mission) vines for personal use, providing a solid base for the future of California winemaking.

Within a decade, Joseph Chapman had rooted about 4000 European vines in Los Angeles, the first such major planting of Old World vines in the New World. Chapman was joined by the Bordelais, Jean Louis Vignes, who rooted large numbers of French vine cuttings in his El Aliso Vineyard in Los Angeles. By the middle of the 19th century, Vinifera had taken a firm hold, nudging California wine into a new era.

During and after the Gold Rush, a hell-raising do-or-die period of American frontier history which lasted from about 1850 to 1860, vineyards prospered throughout the state. Quality and quantity improved quickly, so much so that Charles Kohler and John Frohling, two San Francisco vintners, began to export large lots of premium California wines to England, Germany, Russia, China and Australia.

Inglenook

ESTATE BOTTLED

NAPA VALLEY
CABERNET SAUVIGNON

A full bodied dry red table wine with the distinctive flavor
and aroma of the Cabernet Sauvignon grape variety.

Produced and Bottled by Inglenook Vineyards,
Rutherford, California. Alcohol 12½% by Vol.

ARIZONA

• Escondido

San Diego   MEXICO

Then, in 1857, the man who today is usually called the 'Father of California Winemaking', Colonel Agoston Haraszthy, initiated a change which was to have a major impact on California winemaking. Haraszthy, who apparently came by his military title courtesy of his noble Hungarian lineage, made the switch from Mission to European varieties in a select vineyard experiment in San Diego. Realizing that classic grapes would grow and flourish in California soils, Haraszthy travelled to Europe under an assignment from Governor John G. Downey, to conduct a viticultural search. He returned to his Buena Vista estate in Sonoma with 100,000 cuttings of some 300 varieties. On the long ocean trip from Europe to California, many of the vine identification tags faded or were lost, creating a viticultural puzzle which has yet to be fully solved.

During the decade of the 1860s, Los Angeles, Anaheim and Sonoma became the three major wine and grape regions in the state. By 1870, California had taken over first place as the leading wine producer from Ohio and Missouri.

Two years later, another grape experiment took fruition, eventually changing the face of California winemaking. On a farm near Yuba City, north of Sacramento, William Thompson planted an English hothouse grape. Before a century had elapsed, the Thompson Seedless was one of the most prolific grapes grown in California. Today, despite continuing reports that Thompson Seedless is widely crushed by many California wineries for wine, its use in table winemaking has diminished.

State laws were enacted in 1887 to apply more stringent control over the quality of California winemaking than were required by the federal government. California prohibited the use of sugar and water in winemaking and changed the alcohol requirements for table wines. Production had grown to about 18 million hectolitres (50 million gallons) by the turn of the century, an enormous amount for a young industry that had been wobbling its way along the path of progress on training wheels.

National Prohibition, the great American experiment in collective lunacy, became law in 1920, continuing for thirteen years as one of the most bizarre attempts to legislate morals in the nation's history. By the time Prohibition had reached full tilt, wine production dropped to about 22 million gallons, and wineries began to close by the score. Some established California winemakers like The Christian Brothers, Beaulieu Vineyards, Concannon and others kept their doors open until repeal by producing altar wines. With the Volstead Act of 1933, Prohibition came to an end, but many of the scars left by its oppression remain today.

Federal wine quality and labelling standards became effective in 1936, and Frank Schoonmaker, with the help of a young Alexis Lichine, began touting the use of varietal names on California wines. By the 1950s, perhaps for the first time in their history, Americans began to like wine. Many military people returning home from Europe after two World Wars, had developed a palate for French and German wines. Calls went up in nearly every large city for 'Pooly Foosy'. But at the same time, many newcomers to wines were settling for and enjoying the wines of America. James Zellerbach, at his Hanzell Winery in Sonoma, added another French touch to California wine when he decided to age his 1956 Chardonnay in Burgundian oak. Other winemakers in Sonoma and Napa soon joined Zellerbach, preferring the finesse that French oak imparted to their wine.

Grape varieties

Despite the continued demand for white wine, black grape plantings dominate in California. The ration in 1979 was 68 per cent black to 32 per cent white; white grape acreage is growing, though at a slower rate than the demand for white wine. There are well over 100 varieties planted in California, eighteen of which are major wine grapes. This is the 1979 wine grape acreage breakdown:

Red	White
Zinfandel – 29,884	French Colombard – 35,800
Carignane – 26,555	Chenin Blanc – 27,685
Cabernet Sauvignon – 23,592	Chardonnay – 15,956
Barbera – 20,446	White Riesling – 9,565
Ruby Cabernet – 18,354	Sauvignon Blanc – 6,235
Grenache – 17,477	Palomino – 3,958
Petite Sirah – 13,168	Gewurztraminer – 3,396
Rubired – 11,626	Emerald Riesling – 2,711
Pinot Noir – 9,789	

Producers

The ten largest California wineries are E & J Gallo, United Vintners, Almaden Vineyards, Guild, Paul Masson, Franzia, Sebastiani Vineyards, C.K. Mondavi (Charles Krug), La Mont, and Beringer Vineyards. For a more manageable perspective, the ten can be divided into three groups:
Major three: Gallo, United Vintners (Inglenook), Franzia.
Mid six: Almaden, Masson, Sebastiani, The Christian Brothers, Charles Krug, Beringer Vineyards.
Major premiums: Robert Mondavi Winery, Wente Brothers, Louis P. Martini Winery, Sonoma Vineyards. Souverain Cellars, Mirassou Vineyards, Beaulieu Vineyards.
Providing 2·1 per cent of the total California wine sales, the

major premium wineries, except for Souverain and Sonoma Vineyards, are all family owned; The Christian Brothers is run by the Catholic lay brother teaching order.

The vineyards – climate and soil

Vineyard soils are less of a consideration in US viticulture than climate conditions. This is particularly true in California. But change is taking root as more growers and wine-makers begin to look down instead of up.

When Dr Richard Peterson, winemaker for The Monterey Vineyard, came to northern Monterey County in 1974, he believed that Cabernet Sauvignon would grow there as well as it does in Napa. Such was not the case, as Peterson soon discovered, for that year he made a Cabernet but never released it because of the wine's strong vegetative, green bell pepper intensity, a fact he did not find later in Pinot Noir. Monterey is the coolest of any California region, and such climate, Peterson believes, is ideal for Pinot Noir and Sauvignon Blanc.

Soil compositions vary throughout California. South-east of The Monterey Vineyard, high in the Gavilan mountains, Chalone Vineyards produces highly respected Pinot Noir and Chardonnay from vines in a chalky table. At the base of the Gavilan, where Paul Masson, Wente Brothers and Mirassou Vineyards have huge plantings, the soil is a sandy loam. To the north, in the Napa Valley, where climate conditions are quite different, Diamond Creek Vineyards makes three vineyard-designated Cabernets: Red Rock Terrace, Volcanic Hill and Gravelly Meadow. These are big, gutsy, high tannin wines with assertive personalities, developing from both the soil and the climate.

However, in California, the number of degree-days in a specific geographic region is the system most often used for selecting the right grapes for that area. Operating under the premise that there is a right climate for every grape, but not all grapes will grow well in every climate, University of California-Davis professors, Amerine and Winkler, developed a system in the 1930s of five major growing regions. The university heat summation studies, as the system is called, are based on the fact that wine grapes will not ripen well under 50° F (10°C). The typical growing season in California is 1 April to 31 October. Therefore, during that period, you take the mean temperature (the high and low divided by two) of all days above 50°. This is how the system works. If the high and low temperatures for a particular growing area on a certain day are 90 and 55, the mean for that day is 73. The total of degree-days then is 23 (73-50). From this, the following scale was developed.

California Growing Regions

Region I	2500 degree-days or less
Region II	2501-3000 degree-days
Region III	3001-3500 degree-days
Region IV	3501-4000 degree days
Region V	In excess of 4110 degree-days

Region I climate is similar to northern Burgundy, the Rhine and New York's Finger Lakes. Most of Napa, Sonoma and Mendocino and Monterey south is R-I; ideal for Pinot Noir, Cabernet Sauvignon, Chenin Blanc, and Chardonnay.

Region II climate resembles Bordeaux and Asti, Italy. Napa, Sonoma and Soledad (Monterey) are R-11 areas; good for Cabernet Sauvignon, Riesling, Gamay Beaujolais, Sauvignon Blanc, Merlot and Chenin Blanc.

Region III is similar to Milan, Italy and France's Midi. R-III areas in California include Mendocino, Santa Barbara, Healdsburg and San Diego County; good for Gamay, Barbera, Zinfandel and Semillon.

Region IV climate is like northern Spain, Portugal's Douro Valley and the Mendoza in Argentina, while San Joaquin Valley and northern Sacramento County are R-IV in California; ideal for Mission, Grenache, Palomino, Tinta.

Region V is the hottest, with conditions like North Africa. Here, in the warmest inland valleys, grow the dessert and brandy grapes.

Within all of these five regions are hundreds of microclimates, allowing for even more selective plantings. In Napa Valley, mountain vineyard microclimates like those of Spring Mountain and Mayacamas, differ from the vineyards on the valley floor, and also from the microclimate conditions in the many sub-valleys.

Classification of wines

Federal control over the standards of American wine labelling took hold in 1936, three years after the repeal of Prohibition, with the issuance of the country's first regulations. The latest legislation was issued in August 1979 following a series of hearings in 1976 and 1977. The issuing and controlling agency of the US government is the Bureau of Alcohol, Tobacco and Firearms (ATF), a division of the Department of Treasury.

Today, ATF is a beleaguered agency, attempting at best to cope with problems for which there are no easy solutions.

There are also more mundane regulations for alcohol content, varietal percentage and appellations. The issuance in

1979 of revised regulations will take effect 1 January, 1983. Until then, all California wines listing a grape as the wine name must have at least 51 per cent of that grape in the wine. The other 49 per cent can be just about anything, which is reason enough for an increase to 75 per cent by 1983. Many winemakers, of course, already make 100 per cent varietal wines. If the wine is vintage dated, 95 per cent of it must be from the year stated on the label. This requirement is independent of rules relating to the origin of the grapes.

Geographic origin in wine labelling is a 75-85 proposition. If the appellation is a state or county, 75 per cent of the grapes must come from the designated area. California requires that all wines with 'California' on the label must be 100 per cent from California-grown grapes. If a vineyard designation is used, then the content must be 85 per cent from that vineyard. Multi-county and multi-state *appellations* are allowed so long as they are so stated on the label.

Estate bottled is, perhaps, the least understood and most confusing of wine bottle terms. To qualify for *estate bottled,* the vineyard must be owned, controlled, or leased directly by the winery, though it need not be within eyesight of the winery. Such vague wording has made the value of the term suspect with many vintners. However, by 1983, the winery must be in the viticultural area on the label, and it must own and control the vineyards, and produce and bottle the wine to use 'estate bottled'. Many vintners who now more than qualify for the designation opt not to use it because of the confusion. Others, to avoid the appellation hassle altogether, simply apply general names like California or American.

While varietal wine labels are regulated, generic wine labelling lacks any such control. Federal rules allow for seventeen generic names to be used on American wines: burgundy, chablis, champagne, chianti, claret, hock, madeira, malaga, moselle, port, rhine, sauterne, sherry, and tokay. Winemakers wishing to use these generic names may do so without any consideration for the grapes to be used, or how the wine will be vinted. Not surprisingly, few of these wines bear any similarity to their European namesakes. There is a move, particularly among new wineries, to drop generic names in favour of commonsense ones, like 'table wine'. But the use of generic names continues with many wineries, who cling to the belief that such names are universally accepted, in much the same way that aspirin has become a universal term. Proprietary names and generics which have a passing association with European places continue to linger. Paul Masson Vineyards has for years made a series of soft and easy wines with imaginative names like Baroque and Rhine

Castle. By packaging Baroque in a burgundy-shaped bottle and claiming that it resembles burgundy, Masson gets the job done without using a generic name. The same is not true, however, of Masson Rhine Castle, a fruity white wine in a tall flute bottle that alludes to some undetectable German heritage.

More imaginative label designs and names have emerged lately, mainly from small wineries. Boeger Winery in El Dorado County, makes a blend called Hangtown Red, complete with a Hangman's noose on the label, derived from the area's colourful mining history. In Mendocino, Edmeades Vineyards typifies the essence known in California today as mellow. Edmeades wines carry such unusual names as Whale Wine (part of the sales support the effort to save the whales) and their standard white, Rain Wine, a statement that reflects Mendocino's harvest weather.

Alcohol content in American wines is dependent on the type of wine produced. By law, table wines may vary from 7 to 14 per cent, though most are between 11 and 13 per cent. The recent interest in 'soft' wines has prompted California to lower its minimum alcohol requirement from 10 to 7 per cent. The alcohol percentage on the label may, by law, vary as much as 1·5 per cent on either side of the stated amount. Dessert wines range in alcohol content from 14 to 21 per cent, though most are set at 18 per cent. Sherries cannot have less than 17 per cent alcohol, and no dessert wine may vary more than 1 per cent.

Every California wine label is required to have at least 'bottled by' on the label, a term which can mean either the bottling location, or a corporate address elsewhere in the state other than the place of bottling. It is called DBA or 'doing business as' and in winemaking, DBA is big business. By 1983, though, the address on the label must be the place or location of the actual bottling.

Such terms as 'bottled by', 'cellared by' and 'blended by' mean only that the wine in the bottle was purchased, aged, or blended by the firm. Somewhat better is 'made and bottled by' which indicates that the bottler produced at least 10 per cent of the wine, and also blended the wine in the bottle. The most significant term is 'produced and bottled by', an assurance that the winery has fermented, aged and bottled the wine, and that at least a minimum of 75 per cent is the producer's own wine.

Foreign terms like 'spätlese' are not allowed on American wine labels, but there is no such prohibition on the use of 'cask', 'bin', 'cuvée' and 'mountain' among other label terms which tell the consumer nothing.

For champagne and sparkling wines, there are no legal

127

definitions of such terms as 'brut' and 'extra dry', but a winery producing a sparkler by the Charmat process must show on the label that the wine is 'bulk processed'.

Vintages

An often heard myth about California wine, which has thankfully been laid to rest, is 'every year is a vintage year in California'. Nothing is further from the truth. Weather has always been a key factor in California winemaking, as it has been in other states. California climates vary greatly from the cool coastal counties of Napa, Sonoma and Mendocino, to the hot and arid inland valley of San Joaquin. Ratings shown here are only for the North Coast counties, and do not apply to other growing areas.

1980
Late picking in hot weather yielded low quantities in the Central Coast; quality is very good to excellent throughout, especially for North Coast Chardonnay, Pinot Noir and Cabernet.

1979
Moderate to good year, Cabernet and Chardonnay best, then Zinfandel.

1978
End of long drought yielded very good to outstanding whites, especially Chardonnay.

1977
More drought, light year in North Coast, good in Napa, excellent in Mendocino for reds and Chardonnay and Riesling.

1976
Short crop due to drought, whites better overall than reds; many reds better now than first thought.

1975
Generally light reds, Petite Sirah from Mendocino fared best; very good Napa and Sonoma Chardonnay.

1974
Excellent harvest conditions brought rich, highly flavoured Sonoma and Napa reds. The best need more time and will hold into the 1990s; some good whites.

1973
Very good year for well-balanced Napa Cabernets and Zinfandels; Sonoma reds did very well.

1972
Lowest yields in thirty years; good but not great Napa reds, better in Mendocino, many wines better now than first estimated.

1971
Weak year with poor vintage weather; early ripeners like Pinot Noir holding well.

Though Napa quality was very good in 1970, quantity was cut by about 50 per cent because of spring frosts. Mendocino was hit hardest; best reds outstanding, but others still need time. Other good to superb vintages for red wines: 1969, 1968 (outstanding) and 1966.

NEW YORK STATE

The nature of vine-growing in New York State is as diverse as it is anywhere in the world. Divided into five general viticultural regions, New York vineyards are planted to native varieties, French hybrids and Vinifera. The difference in acreage between Labrusca and Vinifera, though, is great; from a total of nearly 20,000 hectares (50,000 acres) statewide, Vinifera accounts for only about 400 hectares (1,000 acres).

Only two of the regions, Finger Lakes and Chatauqua – both in the western part of the state that is sandwiched between Lake Ontario in the north and Pennsylvania in the south – are major producers. The other three regions are Hudson River Valley, Niagara and Long Island.

Vine-growing in the Finger Lakes region can be traced back to 1829 when Labrusca was first planted in Hammondsport. The first large winery in the region, though, was Pleasant Valley Wine Company, established in 1860, on the shores of Keuka Lake. Six slender lakes make up the Finger Lake chain, but only Keuka, Canandaigua and Seneca are important wine areas.

The wineries

Keuka Lake is home for such major New York wineries as Gold Seal, Taylor Wine Company and Great Western, descendant of the Pleasant Valley Wine Company. Today, Taylor and Great Western are owned by Coca-Cola, while Gold Seal is now under the Seagram umbrella.

Sparkling wines made mostly from the Catawba (Labrusca) and Aurora (hybrid) established these wineries, but each also produces complete lines of table and dessert wines. Taylor and Great Western are the nation's fourth largest producers of wine, while neighbouring Canandaigua Winery and Monarch are eighth and ninth. Gold Seal, third in the area, is also a major sparkling wine firm, but with a French touch.

In the 1930s, Charles Fournier arrived at Gold Seal from Veuve Clicquot-Ponsardin to apply his champenoise style to the wines. Fournier eventually brought other Champagne masters to Gold Seal, setting a tradition still practised today. Gold Seal also planted the first Vinifera in the region in the 1950s, when Fournier gave the 'Mad Russian', Dr Konstantin Frank, the chance to prove that Vinifera would survive the cold winters of upstate New York. Frank, who had come to America from the Ukraine, was called the 'Mad Russian' by Keuka Lake grape growers who did not believe the Vinifera could grow there. Today, Gold Seal makes unique Riesling and (Pinot) Chardonnay; which is added to the cuvée of their Blanc de Blancs champagne among other wines.

129

To date, the Niagara region has no bonded winery, but it is the source of hybrid, Labrusca and Vinifera grapes for table and kosher wines. North-east of New York City, on outer Long Island is the fastest growing wine area in the state. The most active winery in the area is Hargrave Vineyard.

New York State allows its wineries to add both water and sugar to their wines, and up to 25 per cent out-of-state wine. Most of it arrives in railroad tank cars from California and is then added to Labrusca wines to make them more pleasing to the palate. The amelioration is permitted to compensate for the low sugar/high acid grapes of the region. Because of its intense character, Labrusca wine will not be required to meet the 75 per cent minimum when the law changes in 1983.

Grape varieties

Vintaging in New York vineyards is done mainly by mechanical harvesters, though vineyards where terrain is too steep and difficult for a machine to manoeuvre and some small estate vineyards are still hand picked. The following are the major native grapes used for table, sparkling and dessert wines. Since the grapes are used interchangeably, red and white varieties are listed together.

CONCORD The most widely planted variety, it is fairly

low in sugar, but high in Labrusca character.

DELAWARE A good ripener, it has the lowest Labrusca character and is used mainly for white wines.

CATAWBA Names for the Catawba River in North Carolina, it has become the workhorse grape of New York. High in sugar and low in acid, it is a good base for all types of wine.

NIAGARA A Concord-type grape with pronounced Labrusca character.

ISABELLA A red, strongly scented variety used mostly for rosés.

French hybrids were first introduced into the United States in the 1930s by Philip Wagner at his Boordy Vineyard in

Maryland. Since then, interest in hybrids has grown slowly but steadily, as many of these hardy grapes are easier to grow and do not show as much of Labrusca's assertive muskiness. Hybrids generally bear an identifying number, but the wines have been given proprietary names (often incorporating the name of the hybridizer) for easy consumer identification.

White Hybrids
AURORA (Seibel 5279). A widely planted hybrid, it yields a soft and fragrant wine.
SEYVAL BLANC (Seyve Villard 5276). The most promising of the white hybrids, Seyval is a dry wine with a character not unlike Pinot Blanc.
CAYUGA (NYS 33403). A New York State developed hybrid, it is neutral in character, used mostly for blending, though a few wineries do make a varietal Cayuga.

Red Hybrids
BACO NOIR (Baco 1). Produces a medium wine with a vinous nose and good acidity; capable of bottle ageing.
CHANCELLOR NOIR (Seibel 7053). Generally a blending grape, though, as a varietal it is full-bodied with good colour.
DE CHAUNAC (Seibel 9549). Most promising of the red hybrids, it yields a medium wine with a character much like a young Zinfandel.
CHELOIS (Seibel 10878). Fruitier than Baco Noir, Chelois is a grey wine with some spice and Labrusca overtones.
CASCADE NOIR (Seibel 13053). Often used for rosés, this is made as a varietal by less than ten Eastern wineries. Associated Vintners of Washington State has a Cascade Rosé, one of the few hybrid wines made on the West Coast.

Vintages
Eastern wine growing states like New York, Ohio and Pennsylvania, generally have cold harsh winters which push up grape acids and drop grape sugars. In such years, chaptalization and amelioration are usually necessary. Thus, vintage ratings, other than to show quantities, are somewhat pointless for these areas.

PACIFIC NORTH-WEST AND OTHER STATES
Except for the cold northern tier states like Montana and some of the humid Southern states, growth in wine production elsewhere in the country over the past decade has been healthy.
But it is the Pacific North-west states of Washington and Oregon where the strongest challenge to California's

Vinifera-dominance is the most prominent. Washington is the third largest producer of grapes in the country, though its 8000 hectares (20,000 acres) of vines are fewer than New York's total acreage. Labrusca varieties like Concord have always been a major crop in Washington, supplying juice for various grape products, and for the state's fruit wine business.

WASHINGTON

In recent years, production of premium table wines has shown invigorating growth, particularly from innovative wineries like Château Ste Michelle at Woodinville, outside Seattle. Ste Michelle own Vinifera plots around its show-place winery and in the fertile Yakima Valley, about 160 kilometres west of Woodinville. Ste Michelle's strong suit is white wines, of which Riesling, Gewürztraminer, Sauvignon Blanc, and a dry, earthy Semillon have the most class. There is also a fruity Grenache Rosé. From the 1978 vintage Ste Michelle bottled a Riesling Ice Wine, one of only two commercial ice wines made in this country. Montbray Wine Cellars in Maryland made the first in 1975.

Only Ste Michelle wines are seen in any quantity outside Washington, though smaller wineries like Preston Wine Cellars, Associated Vintners and Hinzerling Vineyards, are now beginning to place their wines in the national market.

OREGON

Oregon is a relative newcomer in the competitive arena of table wines. Today, statewide, there are just over 400 hectares (1000 acres) of Vinifera planted. From these vines some impressive wines are being produced like Pinot Noir, Riesling and Gewürztraminer.

Appellation standards in Oregon are more stringent than any other state, even stronger than the new federal regulations. No generic wines are allowed, and a high 90 per cent is set for varietal content, except Cabernet Sauvignon, which can be 75 per cent. The remaining grapes must be Bordeaux varieties like Cabernet Franc and Merlot.

There are more than twenty wineries along Oregon's temperate western belt that lies between the Pacific Ocean and the Cascade mountains. Most are in the Willamette Valley, south west of Portland. Tualatin Vineyards, a 1900 hectolitre (50,000 gallon) winery with 24 hectares (60 acres) of producing vines, makes delightful dry, light Rieslings and one of the best Gewürztraminers I've tasted outside Alsace. Knudson-Erath, at Dundee, midway down the Willamette, is best known for its Pinot Noir. One of the largest producers in the state, Knudson-Erath farms 32 hectares (80 acres) of vines and has a capacity of 3800 hectolitres (100,000 gallons).

Australia

No general rule can be applied to Australian wines – because it is such a huge country with great variations of climate, the character of its wines differs greatly too.

The wines can best be described by taking each State and looking at the wine produced in the different wine-growing areas, though most of the wines are sold under the name of the grape variety. The method of classifying wines is the same throughout Australia.

Classification of wines

Most table wines are sold under the name of the grape variety – Riesling, Semillon, Cabernet Sauvignon – although names like Claret, Burgundy, Chablis and Sauternes are sometimes used. Fortified and sparkling wines are copies of European names. The name of the district is appearing more on the labels of most vintners; for example, Penfold's Bin 128 Coonawarra Shiraz 1976. The use of bin numbers denoting a continuing style of wine is a feature of Australian labelling. Thus there is a Penfold's Bin 128 1976, a Bin 128 1975, a Bin 128 1974, and so on. Not all companies follow this style, however. For example, Kidman's Coonawarra 1976 gives essential information on the front label – maker's name, type of wine (red), district and vintage year. A back label says that the wine is made from blending wines made from Shiraz (Syrah) and Cabernet Sauvignon grapes.

1. Swan Valley
2. Kenwick
3. Margaret River – Busselton
4. Mt. Barker
5. Clare Watervale
6. Murray Valley
7. Springton Eden Valley
8. Barossa Valley
9. Adelaide Environs
10. Reynella, McLaren Vale
11. Southern Vales
12. South East
13. Coonawarra
14. Drumborg
15. Great Western
16. Marong
17. Goulburn
18. N.W. Victoria
19. N.E. Victoria Valley – Rutherglen
20. N.E. Victoria Valley – Milawa
21. Riverina
22. Forbes
23. Mudgee
24. Rooty Hill
25. Hunter Valley
26. Roma
27. Coastal Ranges Vineyards

WESTERN AUSTRALIA

Perth

Fremantle

Great Red Wine of Coonawarra 1976

Terra Rossa Wines Ltd.
Coonawarra

750 ml   PRODUCE OF AUSTRALIA

134

NEW SOUTH WALES
Riverina District

This is by far the largest wine producing area of the State. It is situated on the Murrumbidgee River around the towns of Griffith and it was chosen as an agricultural site by the N.S.W. Government in the early part of this century because of the huge area of fine alluvial soil and the possibility of its being extensively irrigated by the river which is constantly being fed with melting snow from the Great Dividing Range to the east. Natural rainfall is very low and during the long summer, when there is no cover from cloud, the days reach temperatures of up to 40°C over a long period. It is a plain formed by floods and wind-blown soil, and so is fairly flat with low undulating rises.

The great heat and fertile soil together with plentiful water combine to produce very healthy grape vines with large berries of various varieties – Shiraz (Petit Syrah), Riesling, Chardonnay, Semillon and Cabernet Sauvignon, with a number of new (to Australia) varieties being developed.

The smallholdings are owned by individual farmers who sell their produce to large wineries located in the district. Dry white and red wines are produced in enormous quantities and sold largely for the bulk trade, in 2-litre and 4-litre containers. Fortified wines such as 'port', 'sweet sherry', 'dry sherry' and muscat and wines flavoured with fruit juices are popular and have a large sale throughout eastern Australia.

HUNTER VALLEY DISTRICT

This is the quality area of NSW. The Hunter flows from the Great Dividing Range eastward to Newcastle on the coast, about 33°S. At such a latitude one would expect very high temperatures but in fact these are modified by cool winds from the ocean in summer and very heavy cloud cover in the ripening season. The consequence is that the number of degree-days and light hours is similar to that which can be found in the Burgundy area in France and the wines are of a similar high quality.

The area is subject to an unusually large number of natural hazards – torrential rain at harvest time, hail storms which destroy the crops, floods, bushfires, numerous pests and various vine diseases which make the growing of vines very expensive and the yield from the vines very low.

The white wines are soft and develop great flavour after a few years in bottle. They approximate to white burgundies of France but have a highly distinctive character of their own.

The reds are, on the whole, soft and tend to be light. After a few years in bottle they improve enormously and develop a strong flavour which is not reminiscent of any European area. The best of the reds are big-bodied with enormous flavour. Those made from Cabernet Sauvignon and aged in French oak are similar to wines from Bordeaux. Shiraz (Petit Syrah) for the reds and Semillon for the whites are by far the most successful and popular varieties but a great deal of experimenting is being done with Pinot Noir, Merlot, Chardonnay, Riesling, Sauvignon Blanc and Traminer, all of which has proved successful.

Most of the estates produce, bottle and market their wines under their own labels, even though some of them are extremely small. The larger producers, and hence those whose wines are more likely to be available, are Lindeman's, McWilliam's, The Rothbury Estate, Tyrrell's, Tulloch's and Hungerford Hill.

VICTORIA
North-Eastern Victoria

This region sits in a triangle between the highest peaks of the Great Dividing Range to the south and east, the Murray River to the north and the Goulburn Valley to the west. There is enough natural rainfall, the soil is fertile and yields are average (about 4 tonnes to the acre). The quality of the wines is very high particularly the fortified wines from the Rutherglen district on the Murray and the dry whites and reds from Milawa and the Warby range to the south of the triangle, where hills provide slopes which protect the vines from the hot afternoon summer sun.

Central Victoria

The gently undulating country near the Great Divide has a long hot summer, plentiful rainfall and good soil, combining to provide ideal conditions for rich red wine and full-bodied whites. Two or three small makers produce exclusive 'boutique' wines of high quality and distinctiveness in this area.

South-West Victoria

There are 'boutique' wineries – that is, small individually owned plots with wineries operated solely by the owners all through this area. South of the Great Divide is a 'cool climate' zone. Cool summers and cloudy skies make for a long ripening period and extremely high quality wines, both red and white. At Great Western, near the large town of Ararat, one of the 'giants', Seppelt's, make the famous and excellent Great Western Champagne (so called). Château Remy, owned by Remy Martin of France, has a vineyard at Avoca in the hilly country not far from Great Western. Here a superb 'champagne' and high quality red and white table wines are made.

Yarra Valley

The nearest vineyard area to the city of Melbourne, the Yarra Valley is also the best in Victoria and produces minute quantities of exclusive and delicious white wines from Riesling, Chardonnay and Traminer varieties, and elegant, flavourous and highly distinctive reds from Cabernet Sauvignon, Pinot Noir and Petit Syrah varieties.

Geelong area

About an hour's drive from Melbourne and on the fringes of the large city of Geelong, about seven 'boutique' wineries operate, most them in the valley of the Moorabool river. This is the most southerly of the mainland grape-growing areas and the wines both red and white are refined, elegant and distinctive with beautiful flavour. Cabernet Sauvignon, Petit Syrah and Pinot Noir are the favoured varieties, with Traminer and Riesling the important types for the whites.

SOUTH AUSTRALIA

This is generally known as the 'Wine State' because of the vastness of its vineyards and its huge production. The largest zone in the state is along the Murray River around the towns of Renmark, Berri and Waikerie, although there are huge plantings at various centres along the river banks almost to the mouth of the river. The vineyards are set upon the flat flood plains of the river. They are watered from the river throughout the whole year. The rich soil, enormous heat in summer and a plentiful supply of water produce large crops of luscious, sugar-filled grapes. The zone is the main supplier of low-cost fortified and table wines to the eastern states.

All the wine 'giants', the large corporate wine companies, draw the bulk of their supplies from this area. Huge co-operatives made up of small lot holders process the grapes and sell the wine in bulk to the sales aggressive large companies, endeavouring to sell as much as they can under their own labels. Smaller privately owned wineries are scattered along the river. A continual stream of fairly high-class bottled wines is fed into the cities from the river areas which are not expensive but have an appealing flavour.

Barossa Valley

Traditionally, this very old wine area set in a narrow stretch of slightly hilly country between the Mt Lofty ranges and St Vincent's Gulf, has produced some of Australia's most famous wines. The famous Penfold's Grange Hermitage is made largely from grapes grown in 'The Valley'. It is renowned mostly for its ability to produce fairly high-quality dry reds of abundant flavour which are made and marketed by some forty medium-to-large wine companies. The giants of the Australian wine world here are Penfold's, Seppelt's, Orlando, Hardy's Yalumba and Kaiser Stuhl (which is a co-operative).

Barossa Ranges

The hills surrounding the valley are full of vineyards which fight for their existence on steep slopes and rocky soils. The summer temperatues are moderate because of the altitude; cloud cover in summer reduces the light hours and a long cool ripening period is the result. Extremely attractive Riesling-style wines are made, slightly austere and steely when they are dry and a little acidic and sweet when they are 'late-picked'. The reds are inclined to be full-bodied and rich with abundance of flavour, yet with a firm finish. Around the township of Clare, Heinz (canned foods) own a winery known as Stanley and have considerable success in the quality red and white table wine sections of wine shows throughout Australia. Remy Martin own the Quelltaler vineyard and winery which produces wines with a wide following throughout the eastern states. A number of smaller, privately-owned wineries nestle among the valleys and make elegant reds and whites in small quantities.

Southern Vales

This is the area south of Adelaide between the Mt Lofty ranges and St Vincent's Gulf to the point where the ranges abruptly cut off the arable areas and form a rocky knob called Kangaroo Island.

Southern Vales is the area of small wineries and big wines. At its centre is the township of McLaren Vale around which, on the floor of the valley and in the surrounding hills, are about forty vineyards and wineries. Two of these, Hardy's and Wynn's, are the giants and the rest are small, sometimes almost 'home' winemakers. The reds of the districts are fabled – huge, deep-coloured, soft wines with enormous and memorable flavour, extremely agreeable and attractive, though perhaps too strong in flavour for those accustomed to European wines. The whites, on the other hand, are light and delicate with excellent flavour. Grape varieties for the reds are almost entirely Cabernet Sauvignon and Petit Syrah, and for the whites Riesling and Palomino, with 'new' varieties such as Chenin Blanc and Sauvignon Blanc now being planted.

South-East South Australia

The predominant area is Coonawarra, which many of Australia's wine connoisseurs consider produces the country's best red wines. It is only about 3·25 kilometres wide and 14·5 kilometres long, entirely based on a red loam soil *(terra rossa)* with an underlying strata of limestone rock. Beneath this is a never-ending supply of pure water which is tapped by the roots of the vines. The high latitude (37°S, which is equivalent to about 45°N in Europe, as regards climate), heavy cloud cover and cool winds from the nearby southern ocean create conditions of degree-days and sun hours almost identical with Bordeaux. The vines grow prolifically and bear heavily, but crops are restricted to retain quality in the grapes. Petit Syrah and Cabernet Sauvignon grapes are made into separate wines and usually sold separately under varietal labels, although one maker, Kidman, blends the wines and markets them only as 'great red wine of Coonawarra'. The giants, Lindeman's, Wynn's, Penfold's, and Mildara, dominate the area but five or six small makers are popular because of their individual styles.

A comparatively small number of whites are made, generally from Riesling grapes. They are light, fairly high in acidity and develop intense flavour. The late-picked varieties are most attractive, retaining their high acidity and pronounced flavour. A little further north than Coonawarra, at a latitude of about 36°S, is the area known as Padthaway in the electoral district of Keppoch. Although so close, its wines are vastly different to those of Coonawarra. The soil is a sandy loam with a subsoil of clay. There is an underground water supply but no layer of limestone rock. It does not get the cool southerly winds and is hotter in summer than the more southern area. The red wines are bigger, softer and perhaps more flavoursome than Coonawarra reds. The whites are round and soft with a very distinct and prominent flavour. Hardy's, Seppelt's, Lindeman's, and Wynn's own all the vineyards and very often the wines are used as blending material with wines from other areas.

WESTERN AUSTRALIA

The bulk of this State's vineyards extend along the banks of the Swan river (and its tributary, the Canning) which rises in the shallow hills to the east of the city of Perth and flows through the city to the coast at Fremantle. Table wine has been made from Syrah, Cabernet Sauvignon, Chenin Blanc, Semillon and Riesling. Swan Valley fortified wines are of a very high standard, with a liqueur-like quality, and are much sought after by local Western Australians.

The dry table wines are difficult to make because of the excess sugar in the grapes. The reds are inclined to be heavy and sweetish with a pronounced berry flavour. The whites tend to be full-bodied and richly flavoured. Nonetheless, they are very attractive wines and appeal to most wine drinkers in Australia because of their strong flavour and softness.

The planting at Gin-Gin, 80 kilometres north of Perth, are more recent. The whites, particularly, develop a 'tropical fruit' flavour and are most attractive.

Enormous plantings have taken place at Margaret River, just north of the town of Busselton. This is situated on a piece of Western Australia, about 130 kilometres south of Perth, which juts out into the Indian Ocean. High-quality whites and reds are being produced here, mostly under the names of small makers such as Cullity and Pannell, two medical men, and a number of others who took up growing grapes more as a hobby than as a living. There is one large company in the area – Sandalford, which has been making wine in the Swan Valley for over a century.

QUEENSLAND

In recent years a number of 'boutique' wineries have been set up, closer to Brisbane than Roma, in the hills which form a coastal range fairly close to the Pacific Ocean. The cool sea breezes and the altitude make for fairly good conditions for growing table wines. They are small enough to exist on cellar-door sales and their wines, both red and white, have been well received in Brisbane although the more southern cities have not so far been particularly enthusiastic about Queensland wines.

South Africa

Apart from a small production of table wines in the Orange Free State, South Africa's wine industry is based entirely in the Cape Province.

Each year about half the Cape grape harvest goes for distillation into brandy, and a fair proportion of the remainder is used for South African sherries and South African ports. But enough good wine remains to supply a thriving domestic market and rapidly increasing orders from abroad.

The near perfect climate, the moderating influence of the Atlantic ocean and the dramatic coastal mountain ranges, plus a winemaking tradition over three centuries old, have concentrated the premium wine areas along the coast, inland from Capetown and centred on the twin towns of Stellenbosch and Paarl. Further inland, where the summers are hotter and rain less plentiful, the vineyards need irrigation, and the wines tend to go for distillation and conversion into fortified wines. However, in recent years the introduction of sophisticated winemaking techniques have meant that these hotter areas have been able to enter the table wine market with good results.

Classification of wines

In 1972 a profound change came over the whole industry when the Wine of Origin Superior (WOS) laws were enacted. Basically, they set out to establish what could roughly be compared to France's Appellation Contrôlée laws by laying down criteria of quality.

Area of origin

The relatively simple system, which became law on 1 September 1973, first defined and designated the fourteen main grape growing areas: Constantia, Durbanville, Stellenbosch, Paarl and Swartland, all of which can come under the wider designation Coastal Region; Paarl and Tulbagh coming together under the name Boberg for the production of fortified wines only; Tulbagh as a designated winegrowing area; Paarl, Tulbagh, Worcester, Robertson and Swellendam as separate entities or under the broader heading of Breede River; Piletberg, Olifants River, Little Karoo and Overberg, which with Worcester and Robertson constitute the outer vineyard areas.

Varietal name

The third criteria concerns the use of a varietal name. For Cabernet Sauvignon or Pinotage to be used on the label, for example, the wine must have a minimum content of that grape. By the 1984 harvest it will be 75 per cent.

SOUTH AFRICA

Estates If a wine has one of these defined areas on the label it must be made from grapes grown exclusively in that area. And within this system the authorities singled out the very best properties and allowed them to use the word 'Estate' on the label. A South African estate is a smallish wine farm, usually privately owned, which has its own winemaking and cellaring facilities, though it need not bottle its own wine. These estates are the peak of the Cape wine industry, and jealously guard their reputations.

Vintage The second WOS criteria is that if a vintage is to be used on the label, it must be only the wine of that year.

A producer who wishes to obtain a Wine of Origin certificate must meet these requirements in part or full. To get the better designation Wine of Origin Superior, the wine must pass analytical and tasting tests by a panel of experts.

The seals are issued by the Wine and Spirit Board and affixed to the capsule with a specific number for each bottle so the wine can be traced. At the top of the seal will be 'Estate' if the wine so qualifies. Then, from top to bottom, horizontal blue, red and green stripes denote area of origin, vintage and variety (known as *cultivar* in South Africa) as described on the label. At the bottom will be Superior if the wine has passed all its tests.

A wine may be blended, and though it still passes through rigorous controls, it will only get the area of origin and vintage bands because it is made from more than one grape variety – but it *can* get the Superior designation.

This WOS seal has become the cornerstone of the Cape wine industry, automatically telling the consumer the wine is a class ahead of the pleasant, well-made everyday drinking wines sold in large quantities. By this legislation and by agreement among the growers, the Cape wine industry is one of the most tightly legislated in the world.

142

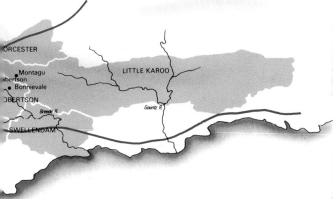

Grape varieties

The coastal area soils are mainly sand with decomposed granite closer to the mountains, while further inland the soils are redder, alluvial and granitic. The only grape native to the area is Pinotage, a red wine variety, which was developed by Professor A.I. Perold in 1925 by crossing Pinot Noir and Cinsaut (or Hermitage, hence the name). It is one of the main red wine grapes, the others being Cabernet Sauvignon, Shiraz and Cinsaut, all originally imported from France. The Cinsaut is used for making South African port and for blending to soften young Cabernet Sauvignon, but in the best areas it is now gradually being replaced as a premium red table wine grape.

Other important red wine grapes are Tinta Barocca, originally from Portugal's Douro valley and, as in Portugal, widely used for making fortified wines but also yielding some interesting full red wines; Grenache, Pinot Noir, Gamay; newer plantings of Malbec and Merlot which some growers plan to use to make lighter, more claret-style wines to compete against the traditional heavier style of red wine;

143

and some very new plantings of the Californian Zinfandel.

The most popular white cultivar is the Steen grape, one of the earliest vines planted and till recently, when it was identified as the Chenin Blanc of France, thought to be a local hybrid. It yields a fresh, fruity wine that often has a residual sweetness, and is also left late on the vine to concentrate the sugar and give 'Late Harvest' semi-dessert wines. In South Africa it can be designated Chenin Blanc, Steen or Stein on the label.

The other main white grape is the Semillon or Greengrape, giving a dry white wine which is often blended with a little Steen to add a touch of sweetness. Both are now being increasingly replaced in the best growing areas by the Sauvignon Blanc and Chardonnay from France, giving fresh dry wines of a higher overall quality and complexity, roughly equatable to their respective French counterparts from the Loire and Burgundy.

As in other parts of the world, the swing in South Africa has been to white wine drinking, partly due to the traditional heaviness of the reds. Pinotage, Cabernet, Shiraz and Tinta all yield heavy rich wines that improve greatly with age, but which are hard to drink when young, particularly in the warm South African climate.

Wine producers

The three big groups of South Africa's wine industry are: the Ko-operatieve Wijnbowers Vereniging (KWV), the Oude Meester Group, and Stellenbosch Farmers' Winery (SFW).

The KWV, founded in 1918 when the Cape wine industry was at a low ebb, was created to look after the interests of the wine farmers. It still does, and membership is obligatory for each wine-grape grower. It has the decisive role in, for example, fixing minimum grape prices, advising the government on legislation affecting the wine-grape growers, and its definitive role in research and development.

The KWV is not allowed to market wine within South Africa, but can do so abroad. In recent years it has built up markets for Cape sherries and Cape ports under KWV, Edward Cavendish, and private labels, and has extended its influence into table wine markets with labels like the red blended Roodeberg and KWV Chenin Blanc.

The Oude Meester group, by a unilateral decision between the big three, now dominates the domestic market for wine, as the head of a Cape consortium. Its main labels are the Fleur du Cap and Grunberger ranges, Drostdy fortifieds, and the wide spread of estate producers whom the company represents in the market. The SFW has as its main labels the Nederburg range, the blended Baronne and Duette, Monis fortifieds, and Libertas wine.

Argentina

The present area of viticulture is at the foot of the Andes mountains and extends from the Tropic of Capricorn to 40°S. Altogether there are 350,000 hectares under vine, 72 per cent of which are in the province of Mendoza, 18 per cent in San Juan province, 5 per cent in the Rio Negro area in the extreme south, and the rest spread throughout the northern provinces of La Rioja, Catamarca and Salta.

Climate and soil

Apart from the Rio Negro area, the land is semi-desert with a very low annual rainfall of 150-250 millimetres. The clear, dry air reduces risk of disease of the vine and the very high summer temperatures of up to 40°C guarantee large, even vintages. All the vineyards are flat and irrigated by an intricate system of reservoirs, canals and ditches introduced by the early settlers. The water comes from the everlasting snow on the peaks of the high Andes and, more recently, from deep bore holes which have led not only to increased production, but also to extensive afforestation that gives much needed shade to the vines during the hot summer months. As one would expect, the soil is of a loose, sandy nature, with sub strata of clay. Vines are trained according to the type of grape and the quality of wine required; over 50 per cent of the vineyards employ the European low or high espalier system, but in the hotter areas, the parral cuyano, or trellis method, is gaining ground.

The vineyards

The vineyards are made up of smallholdings whose owners sell their grapes to the big bodegas and co-operatives. For instance, there are more than 32,000 separate vineyards in the province of Mendoza alone. The vintage starts in early February and lasts until mid-April. In the main, itinerant labour is used for picking, although mechanical harvesters are being introduced gradually, as new vineyards are planted. The big bodegas can handle up to 2,500,000 kilograms of grapes a day, with their ultra-modern crushing, destalking and fermenting equipment. Annual yields average 27,000,000 hectolitres, making Argentina the fourth biggest wine producer in the western world.

Classification of wines

Argentina also has the third highest domestic consumption of wine in the world, so much of the production is devoted to brands of ordinary wine, or vino de mesa. The prolific Criolla Grande, a derivative of the grape variety brought by the Jesuits, accounts for 25 per cent of the total yield, but with

145

the growing demand for better wines, the use of varietals such as the Cabernet Sauvignon, Malbec, Pinot Noir, Barbera, Tempranillo, Chardonnay, Pinot Blanc, and Riesling is on the increase. All aspects of planting, production, labelling and the movement of wine are supervised by the Instituto Nacional Vitivinicultura (NVA). In the past, generic European names like 'Margaux', 'Chablis' and 'Val de Loire' have been used on labels, but this practice has now been restricted. Nevertheless, the big sparkling wine producers still call their wine 'Champaña'.

The wines

Irrigated vineyards cannot claim to produce the very finest wine, but Argentine producers have greatly improved their methods of production in recent years, so that their varietals compare favourably with their European counterparts in the medium price range. Because of the climate, vintages vary very little from year to year, but a good Cabernet Sauvignon from Mendoza will display the deep red colour, the tannin and firmness of finish that one associates with this grape. White wines, too, now have more fruit, freshness and acidity as a result of early picking, careful selection and the use of cold fermentation.

Producers and shippers

Among the best known firms, some of whom export their wines, are Peñaflor (owners of the excellent Andean Vineyard and Trapiche range to be found in the UK and USA), Gargantini, Pascual Toso, Bodegas Bianchi, Suter and Norton, Lopez, Rural and M. Chandon (the Champagne firm). There are also excellent brands of Argentine wine bottled in the UK under the names of Franchette and Estancia, that have received glowing commendations from the trade and wine writers, because of their excellent value for money.

Brazil

Although the first vineyards were started by Portuguese colonists on the coastal plain, today's centre of viticulture, instigated by Italian immigrants, is about 150 kilometres from Porto Alegre in the cooler mountain areas of the Rio Grande do Sul. To the Italians who poured into the state in their thousands during the 1870s, it was as if they had found a home from home. Sixty-five per cent of the total production comes from around the towns of Bento Gonçalves, Garibaldi and Caxias, but a big vineyard area has recently been developed at Sant'ana do Livramento near the Uruguay border. In all, there are 70,000 hectares under vine.

Climate and soil
The very humid summers render winemaking difficult; there is always plenty of sugar in the grapes, but acidity is low. The reddish, sandy topsoil covers a heavy stratum of clay which makes careful wine selection essential.

The vineyards
The high espalier system of training predominates; many of the vineyards are terraced as the slopes are steep. The vintage starts in early January and runs until late February.

Classification of wines
Because of climatic conditions, most vineyards are planted with American hybrids, with the Isabella grape by far the most common. However, since several multinational corporations took an interest in the area during the 1970s, there has been a switch back to European varieties, with the Cabernet Franc, Merlot, Barbera, Syrah, Trebbiano, and Riesling leading the way. Most Brazilian wines are blends sold domestically under brand names, but there is now a move to export varietals.

The wines
Those made from hybrids have a characteristically 'foxy' smell and flavour and even Vinifera wines have a common 'gout de terroir'. However, recently the quality has improved, and a Brazilian red wine tasted at the 1979 World Wine Fair at Bristol won much acclaim.

Producers and shippers
The leading firms are the Cooperativa Vinicola Aurora, the Compania Vinicola Rio Grandense and Dreher SA who are owned by the Heublein Corporation in the USA. Firms like National Distillers, Cinzano, Martini and Moet & Chandon have also established themselves. Dreher's Marjolet is one of the best red wines in South America.

Chile
Chile is nearly 5000 kilometres long and at no point more than 320 kilometres wide. The vineyards, covering approximately 10,000 hectares, extend from 27°N to 39°S, a distance of 1440 kilometres, but they all have three features in common: the Andean mountain range to the east, the Pacific Ocean with its cold Humboldt Current to the west, and the searing heat of the Atacama Desert to the north – natural barriers which undoubtedly prevented that scourge of the vine, phylloxera, from reaching Chile.

There are six main areas of production, but the Central

Valley zone between the Aconcagua and Maule rivers is by far the most important, both from the quantity (52 per cent) and quality viewpoints. The best wines come from the Maipo Valley near the capital, Santiago.

Climate and soil

Rainfall varies from near zero in the North Central zone to over 1000 millimetres per annum in the southern viticultural zone. Most of the best vineyards are irrigated, the land is flat and the soil varies from sandy to limestone, ideal for growing the Cabernet Sauvignon. Summers are hot and dry.

The vineyards

Since the modern Chilean wine industry began in the 1850s, French influence has been strong. Guyot pruning is used on the low and high espalier methods of training, but the parral system is being introduced gradually, as new areas are released by the authorities for the cultivation of the vine. The harvest starts in February and lasts approximately six weeks.

Classification of wines

Chile's equivalent to Argentina's Criolla, the Païs, is still widely used for the production of vino común in the northern and southern zones. In the Central Valley zone, it is the Cabernet Sauvignon that by tradition predominates, along with the Cabernet Franc, Merlot and Cot. More demand for white wine has led to the planting of Pinot Chardonnay, Sauvignon, Sémillon, and Riesling.

The wines

Chilean red wines, particularly those from the Cabernet Sauvignon, can be spectacularly good, but one suspects that this is due as much to the natural benefits as to the skills of the winemaker. Because of the intransigence of successive governments, the industry is undercapitalized and poorly equipped; too much emphasis is placed on ageing in wood and white wines have, in the past, tended to oxidize. However, with the need to export now an increasing necessity, the quality of all wines is being slowly improved.

Producers and shippers

The most famous Chilean estate is Cousiño Macul, and its Antiguas Reservas Cabernet compares favourably with many good Bordeaux. So does the Cabernet from the small firm of Viña Linderos. Other firms of note are Concha y Toro SA, who have a big following in the USA, Viña Undurraga SA, Viña Santa Rita SA, Viña Santa Carolina SA, Viña de José Canepa and Bodegas San Pedro.

Austria

The viticultural area of Austria is made up of four regions which are then broken down into many wine districts. The largest region is Lower Austria followed by Burgenland, Styria and Vienna. Nearly two thirds of the wine produced comes from Lower Austria, which is made up of eight districts The Wachau, Krems, Langenlois, Klosterneuburg, Falkernstein, Retz, Gumpolskirchen and Vöslau. The Burgenland is the second largest area, with the districts of Rust-Neusiedlersee and Eisenberg. Styria is divided into three districts, South Styria, West Styria and Kloch-East Styria. The smallest region is Vienna where the vineyards extend into the city limits of this famous cultural centre.

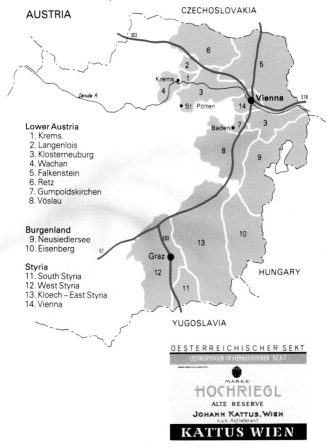

AUSTRIA

CZECHOSLOVAKIA

303

Krems

Danube R.

St. Pölten

Vienna

E16

Baden

Graz

HUNGARY

YUGOSLAVIA

Lower Austria
1. Krems
2. Langenlois
3. Klosterneuburg
4. Wachan
5. Falkenstein
6. Retz
7. Gumpoldskirchen
8. Vöslau

Burgenland
9. Neusiedlersee
10. Eisenberg

Styria
11. South Styria
12. West Styria
13. Kloech – East Styria
14. Vienna

OESTERREICHISCHER SEKT

ERSTKLASSIGER OESTERREICHISCHER SEKT

MARKE:

HOCHRIEGL

ALTE RESERVE

JOHANN KATTUS, WIEN
k.u.k. Hoflieferant

KATTUS WIEN

The Austrian system of cultivation changed dramatically in the 1950s with the introduction of the High Culture method invented by the grower Lenz Moser of Rohrendorf.

Grape varieties

Austria produces predominantly white wines, 84 per cent white and 16 per cent red, the country's production is of 98 per cent quality wines, because of the warm dry climate and sunshine in the early autumn they are able to yield full fruit wines, and in the region of the Burgenland excellent Beeren-auslesen and Trockenbeerenauslesen.

The most important grape variety is the Grüner Veltliner which is only to be found in Austria, and being 31 per cent of the country's entire harvest, is to be found in all the wine growing regions producing a light, fruity, spicy wine.

The vineyards

A good 50 per cent of the vineyards are owned by small farmers with about 12 acres, a further 45 per cent own between 12 and 15 acres. Many of the small growers in specific regions market their harvest through Wine Growers Co-operatives, (Winzergenossenschaft) thereby giving them the guarantee of economical survival. However, there are very many small growers firmly established and producing very fine wines under their own brand names.

Falkenstein and Retz have the record for the most sunshine hours and the district of Retz has the lowest rainfall in Austria, and produce some of the finest wines, light fruity suitable for everyday drinking. The district of Gumpolds-kirchen also produce excellent wine, the most prestigious is the "konigswein" which before it qualifies to be called so, must be submitted to a tasting commission. The district of Vöslau is centered around the spa town of Bad Vöslau and Wiener Neustadt to the south. Apart from the red wines produced here Vöslau is well known for its production of sparkling wine.

The wines from Burgenland are in the main white, and the many small growers produce some of the finest dessert wines in Austria, Spätlese, Auslese, Beerenauslese and Trockenbeerenauslese are of the highest quality and occasionally one can come across an Eiswein. There is better vinification in Burgenland, much less sulphur in the wine. The wines are lighter and have more bouquet.

From Kloch-East Styria comes the best Gewürztraminer. Very little red wine is produced, and in South Styria are some of the highest situated vineyards in the world at 1800 feet.

The Schilcher wines which come in different colours – the darkest red grows in Ligist, the light reds to rose from Stainz and their colour resembles the colour of onion skin – are called Zwiebel Schilchers. The wine is thin and acid.

Switzerland

In terms of wine production, Switzerland is not an important country, but the Swiss enjoy drinking wine. As a result, little of their wine is seen outside the country.

VAUD

The greatest wines of Switzerland are made along the northern shores of Lake Geneva from the Chasselas grape, which is called the Dorin. The vineyards begin in the Rhône Valley, just to the west of Geneva. There is the most important vineyard village of Switzerland, Satigny, though its wines have no great reputation. By the lake, the vineyards are steeply terraced and benefit from the reflected sunlight. The main regions, from west to east, are Mandement, Vaud, Lavaux and Chablais; the best wines of all probably come from the village of Dézaley, just to the east of Lausanne. The city itself has an important vineyard holding there, and the best-known vineyard is Clos de l'Arbalète. Other neighbouring villages with a good reputation include Grandvaux, Lutry and Saint-Saphorin. Further to the east, where the Rhône enters the lake, are Yvorne and Aigle, which also produce good, light, crisp white wines. A little red wine is made under the name of Salvagnin. Testuz is one of the more reliable merchant's names to look for.

VALAIS

The Rhône valley from Sion to Brig is the sunniest and driest part of Switzerland. Here the Chasselas is called the Fendant and produces much more meaty wines than in Vaud. Also grown in the region are the Sylvaner, which is confusingly called the Johannisberg and the Malvoisie, or Pinot Gris. For red wines, which are called Dole, the Pinot Noir and the Gamay are used. One speciality is the *glacier* wine, which is aged for up to fifteen years in casks made of larchwood.

NEUCHATEL

This area, around the Lac de Neuchâtel, in the north-west of Switzerland, produces both red and white wines. The former are made from the Pinot Noir and the latter, which are bottled often without filtration to leave a little sparkle in the wine, from the Chasselas.

TICINO

Most Swiss red wine is made in the Italian-speaking part of the country to the south around the towns of Bellinzona, Locarno and Lugano. Though quite a lot of it is produced, the fact that it is not mentioned in a government booklet on the wines of the country speaks for itself.

Yugoslavia

As early as the 6th century B.C., Greek colonists along the Dalmatian coast were making such good wine that they exported to other Adriatic colonies. The Romans who followed expanded the area under vine inland, and by the time of Domitian (A.D. 81-96) they were banned from making certain types of wine to protect the Italian grape growers from 'foreign' competition.

The modern Yugoslav wine industry is based on a string of semi-autonomous co-operatives which compete vigorously against each other for domestic and export markets. All vinify wine, but only the big ones bottle and market the product. These key co-operatives are based in the big cities: Belgrade, Dubrovnic, Rijeka, Llubljana.

The vineyards stretch around the Yugoslav borders, along the whole of the Adriatic coast and its islands, south of Skopje to the Greek border, north into Serbia along the Bulgarian border, and from Belgrade via the Fruska Gora area to Ljutomer in the north-east, bordering Austria and Hungary. Only the mountainous central areas of Croatia and Bosna-Hercegovina remain relatively vine free.

Classification of wines

Yugoslav wines are usually named after the grape variety, though the whites in particular are sold abroad under different brand names. The main co-operatives supplying these wines are Navip (Belgrade), Vinoprodukt (Zagreb), Vinag (Maribor), Hepok (Mostar) and Slovinija Vino (Ljubjana).

Yugoslav crno (red wine) comes from the warmer areas along the Dalmatian coast, in the Macedonian south and from Serbia. These wines tend to be big, chunky reds with plenty of personality. Around Rijeka the Teran is the main grape with other plantings of Cabernet and Merlot. From Split to Dubrovnic the Dingac, Postup and Prošek give heavy reds from hot, rocky vineyards, while the Plavac and Plavina make rather lighter wines.

Further south, almost on the Albanian border, Vranac and Plavka give an acceptable claret-style wine. The Kosovo area north-west of Skopje uses Burgundac, Cabernet Franc, and Gamay, while Prokupac and Teran dominate the Macedonian and Serbian vineyards.

Yugoslav whites from the cooler inland areas have reached a higher overall quality than the reds. From the hilly vineyards of Ljutomer and Ormoz, with the Austrian Alps visible on a clear day, and from around Maribor comes the internationally popular Yugoslav Riesling from the Laski-Rizling grape, a light, fresh and fruity white. Other white *(bijelo)* wines are being made from the Rhine *(renski)* Riesling, Sauvignon,

Traminer, and Muscat grapes.

In the Fruska Gora region north of Belgrade the volcanic soils are lending themselves to the planting of Traminer, Semillon and Sauvignon, and a number of hybrids are being tested.

Around Mostar on the coast, Zilavka gives an unusual white combining fruit and acidity, a contrast to the fat unappealing Pošip and Maraština alternatives.

Hungary

No one knows when the art of winemaking first arrived in Hungary, but there are numerous mentions of vineyards there in Roman times, even in that northern part of the country which was beyond the confines of the Empire.

The largest vineyard area nowadays is on the Great Hungarian Plain, a region of very sandy soil suitable for little else but the vine. The climate is severe – basically, there are only two seasons, a hard winter followed by a long hot summer. The Alföld area has about 100,000 hectares of vines, producing light wines which are mainly consumed in Hungary. White wines are made from the Olasz Riesling and a number of other local varieties; red wines are made from the Kadarka. The best-known wines come from Csengöd and Kiskoros.

The next most important area is in the north of the country, centred on the pretty town of Eger, which is noted for its Egri Bikaver, or Bull's Blood. This is a deep red wine which ages exceptionally well. The soil is volcanic in origin and the main grape varieties are the Kadarka, which accounts for about 70 per cent of the blend, the Médoc Noir and the Kefrankos. Nearby an excellent white wine, Hárslevelu of Debro, is made. This is a full-bodied, sweet dessert wine.

The vineyards of Mór, also in the north of the country, owe their existence to a number of Bavarian immigrants at the beginning of the 18th century. The vineyards are planted on a quartz-based soil, which enabled the vineyards to resist phylloxera, and native Hungarian rootstocks are used. The climate is ideal and a sweet white wine, high in alcohol, is made from the Ezerjö grape.

In the extreme north-west of the country lie the vineyards of Sopron. Here a refreshing red wine is made from the Kekfrankos, or Gamay, grape. This vaguely resembles a Beaujolais and is best drunk young.

There is an important vineyard area on the northern shores of Lake Balaton. The soil, which is basically basalt, retains heat well, making for ideal growing conditions. Most of the wine produced is white, made mainly from the Olasz Riesling (a full-bodied, sweet wine), the Pinot Gris, and the drier, spicy Furmint. Not far to the north is the smallest vineyard area in Hungary, Somló. The wines here range from dry table wines to rich dessert wines. They are frequently vintaged and age well. Legend has it that they assist considerably in the production of male children and the Hapsburg archdukes used to take regular doses with this in mind.

Pécs is probably the Hungarian wine seen most often in Britain. It is made in the extreme south-west of the country on the Yugoslavian frontier. The wines are without great pretensions and are made mainly from the Kadarka for red and rosé wines, and the Olasz Riesling for the whites.

If Pécs is the most commonly seen Hungarian wine, Tokay has the greatest reputation. It comes from twenty-five villages in the north-east of the country and has long been known for its medicinal properties. Paracelsus tried to extract gold from it and it became the favourite wine at the courts of Louis XIV and Peter the Great.

As in the Sauternes region, the grapes are allowed to shrivel up, and the harvest does not traditionally start until 28 October, often continuing until the snows of December. The Hungarian word for the description of these ultra-sweet grapes is *aszú*. The highest quality of all Tokays is the eszencia. This is made from the minute quantity of juice which falls from unpressed grapes under their own pressure.

Tokays are normally graded for sweetness by the number of *puttonyo* on the label. These represent the number of butts of *aszú* wine in the overall blend. Whilst theoretically this might range from one to six, in practice it will be from three to five; the more *aszú* the sweeter, and more expensive, the wine.

Tokay Szamorodni wine comes from the same area, but not from individually selected grapes. It can be either sweet or dry, the latter being similar to a light fino sherry.

In production terms, Hungary is not one of the world's greatest wine countries – it ranks but fourteenth. Nevertheless, the range and quality of its wines has given it a deserved reputation. Sixty per cent of the production is white wine and as much as one bottle in eight is a naturally sweet, unfortified dessert wine. As far as foreign markets are concerned, all trade is carried out by the governmental organization Monimpex.

Romania

Of all the East European countries that have tried to penetrate Western markets with their wines, only three have succeeded: Hungary, Yugoslavia and Romania. The success of Romania's range of four Premiat wines in the United States has been all the more exciting when one remembers that, unlike most other successful imported products in that country, there can only have been a minimal ethnic following. The wines have had to stand or fall on their own merits. As well as being able to produce branded wines in vast quantities, Romania has individual vineyard regions which have a long history.

From the beginning of the 14th century, there have been mentions of the vineyards of Cotnari, in Moldavia. Cyrus Redding, in 1833, described the wine as being green, becoming deeper by age; it is 'nearly as spirituous as brandy, and by many preferred to Tokay'. Apparently much of the production was exported to Russia.

The wine most often seen is the Tirnave Riesling, from the Transylvanian plain. There has been much planting here during the last thirty years, in irrigated vineyards. The Riesling is the most generally planted vine, but award-winning wines are also made from the Traminer, the Sauvignon, and the local Feteasca.

To the west, in the areas of Banat and Arad, and to the south round Dragasani and Dealul Mare, red wines are made from the Cabernet Sauvignon, Merlot and Pinot Noir. In the extreme south-east of the country, the thirsts of the Black Sea tourists are slaked by the wines of Murfatlar of which the whites made from the Chardonnay, Italian Riesling and Pinot Gris are particularly good.

As a general rule, the wines of Romania can be relied on. The country is proud of its traditional links with France and the improvement in vinification techniques over the past few years have been noteworthy. On the whole the white wines are rather more appealing than the reds.

Bulgaria

Outside North Africa, there can be few countries in the world which have designed their wine production mainly for export markets. One of those that has is Bulgaria. In 1948, Vinprom was established to rationalize the country's wine industry and since then there have been vast plantings, mainly of western European grape varieties such as the Chardonnay, the Riesling and the Sylvaner for white wines and the Cabernet for red wines. Generally, wines made from local varieties, like the Dimiat and the Gamza, are considerably less interesting. Most of the production is sold to Russia and the Eastern bloc, though it can also be found in Germany under a variety of flowery brand names, such as Klosterkeller and Donau Perle. The Cabernet Sauvignon is widely available in Britain and generally represents excellent value for money, being very true to the grape characteristic.

There are two main vineyard areas in the country – the plain to the south of the river Danube, which marks the frontier with Romania, and the valley of the Maritza river. On the

Danubian plain the vineyards have been planted to make cultivation by machinery easier. Here more ordinary wines are produced. In the Maritza valley, the vineyards are irrigated and a full range of varietal wines are made.

Of the local varieties, white wine without much character is made from the Dimiat, whilst the Rcatzitelli makes something rather fuller in style. Of the reds, the Gamza is fresh and fruity, with some acidity. It is best drunk young. The Misket is still something of a lightweight, but the Mavrud is dark and tannic, benefiting from some time in bottle.

Greece

Though Greece has a vineyard area almost twice as large as that of West Germany, it produces little more than half as much wine. There are two reasons for this: firstly, the average yield of grapes per hectare is much lower in Greece than in Germany; and secondly, a very large proportion of the grapes grown there are dried to be sold as currants or sultanas. However, the entry of Greece into the Common Market will no doubt mean that we shall see many more of her wines on the off-licence shelves. What are we to expect?

Much of the ordinary white table wine, and a little of the rosé, is resinated and sold under the name of retsina. This may appear strange to unsophisticated palates, but there is no doubt that it helps to disguise some of the rather doubtful oil in which Greek food is cooked.

Mavro is a generic term for red wines and these are often more palatable. I have enjoyed the red wine of Naoussa, to the west of Thessalonika in Macedonia, but it is probably safest to buy one of the branded wines from a company like Achaia Clauss – Imperial and Castel Danielis – or Cambas. These, generally, have been adapted for a broader appeal.

The sweet wines of Greece have a wide international sale. The Muscat wine from Samos is popular in France and Germany, and Malvasia is produced throughout the islands of the Aegean Sea. The sweet red wine, Mavrodaphne, is made near Patras on the Peloponnese.

Cyprus

In France, one person in eight lives directly or indirectly from the vine; in Cyprus, almost one in four so gains his living. Vines cover 8 per cent of the surface area of the island in smallholdings.

'Sherry'

Thirty per cent of the wine production is of Cyprus 'sherries'. The warm climate produces wines high in natural sugar and subsequently in alcohol. Traditionally, the fermented wine was left outside in casks to oxidize, but now the more traditional Spanish *solera* system, and the cultivation of *flor* are making for much better wines.

Commandaria is still made in the traditional way. The grapes are picked and then left outside to dry. The juice is then run off for fermentation in tanks or, in some cases, earthern jars called *mana*. These are never emptied, but any wine that is drawn off is replaced – thus the *mana* system is the Cypriot equivalent of the Spanish solera.

Table wines

Though a very large proportion of the grapes grown are sold for table purposes, a great deal of table wine is still made. Irrigation is prohibited, so the grape varieties used have to be drought resistant. The main local varieties are the Mavro for red wines, and the Xynisteri for white wines, with the white Málaga and Sultana and the black Opthalmo in secondary roles. In addition, extensive tests have been carried out with a number of imported species. The most successful species for table wines are the Clairette, Carignan Noir, Shiraz, Grenache, Semillon, Cabernet Sauvignon, and Oeillade.

England

The first point that should be made about English wine is that it is an entirely separate product from British wine. The former is made from fresh grapes from the vineyards of England (there are now one or two in Wales and one on Jersey as well). The latter is made from imported grape concentrate, to which sugar is added. This is then fermented with water to make, more often than not, a port or sherry style wine.

The humid climate and unreliable summers are the main problems facing the English *vigneron* and it is largely the development of new varieties of vine, particularly in Germany, that has led to the rapid increase in the acreage of vineyards in this country over the past few years. One of the first growers to sell his wine in commercial quantities was Major-General Sir Guy Salisbury-Jones. His vineyard at Hambledon in Hampshire owes much to technical assistance from friends in Champagne. On the other hand, the first grower to have taken up winemaking as a full-time occupation, Ken Barlow of Adgestone on the Isle of Wight, has relied more on German expertise.

The most common grape varieties planted are the Müller-Thurgau, Reichensteiner, and Huxelrebe from Germany and the Seyve-Villard and Madeleine-Angevine from France. Almost all the wine is white and the taste, generally speaking, is somewhere between that of the Loire and the lesser varieties of Alsace. Amongst the better producers, whose wines are sold commercially, are Wooton, Wraxall and Pilton Manor from Somerset, Three Choirs from Gloucestershire, Adgestone from the Isle of Wight, Hambledon from Hampshire, Chilsdown from Sussex, Lamberhurst Priory from Kent, Felstar from Essex, and Magdalen from Norfolk.

Algeria

Since the French left Algeria in 1962, the area under vines has been reduced by a third and the production has halved. This graphically illustrates the past role of the wines of the country; in the main, they were designed for blending with the low-strength, rather acid wines of the Midi to produce the daily *six étoiles* of the French consumer. Now Common Market law forbids the blending of wines from outside the Market with those from within.

Perhaps the best Algerian wines come from Mascara, to the south-east of Oran. These can reach a natural strength of 16° and are deep in colour, full-bodied and soft. The region of Dahra is between the Oued Chelif and the coast. There the Grenache is the main grape variety and it makes light-coloured wines, high in alcohol, which quickly takes on the oxidized rancio taste liked by so many Frenchmen. South of Algiers are the vineyards of Medea, where full-flavoured red wines, which age well, are made.

For the Algerian government, there is the conflict between the Moslem laws which prohibit the consumption of alcohol and the need to earn foreign currency. The wines are not what they used to be, but they are getting better all the time. Whilst the exodus of the French may have shattered the reputation of the wines of Algeria; the arrival of the *pieds noirs* in the Midi and in Corsica has done much for the wines of those regions.

Tunisia

Most of the wine is now made by modern techniques in vast co-operative cellars and once again the red and the rosé wines can be palatable, while the whites are generally more disappointing. The main grape varieties planted are the Grenache, the Cinsault and the Carignane for the red wines, and the Ugni Blanc, Clairette and Pedro Ximenez for the white wines. The reputation of Tunisian dessert wines made from the Muscat grape was once considerable, but they are rarely seen outside the country.

The main vineyard area is south of Bizerta and the quality of all wines sold on export markets is supervised by l'Office du Vin de Tunisie.

Glossary

Affenthalera A German red wine from the Baden region characterised by a monkey on the outside of the bottle.

Appellation Contrôlée Top rank French classification guaranteeing quality and origin.

Auslese Quality German wine produced from selected bunches of grapes left to ripen on the vine.

Beerenauslese Quality German wine produced from grapes individually picked from selected bunches.

Botrytis cinerea Or 'noble rot', a type of mould that in warm and humid conditions affects only white grapes in such a way that the natural sugar content of the fruit is increased.

British Wine Wine made in Britain from imported unfermented grape juice.

Chaptalizing Sugaring of the must before or during fermentation to increase alcohol content.

Charmat method or Cuvé Close Or *tank method* where secondary fermentation takes place in a closed tank in the making of sparkling wines other than champagne or those made by *methode champenoise*.

Clavelin A 50cl dumpy bottle used for *vin jaune* made in the Jura.

Corked Either an inferior cork has been used which has affected the flavour of the wine or a weevil has penetrated the cork and air has got into the wine.

Cru Classé wine One of the five official classed growths of Bordeaux.

Degree-days Californian system of grading areas by measuring the amount of sunshine each area receives in order to select the best grape varieties for each area.

Deutsche Prädikatssekt Quality German sparkling wine.

Deutsche Tafelwein German table wine.

DOC (Denominazione di Origine Controllata) Italian classification guaranteeing quality and origin.

DOCG (Denominazione di Origine Controllata e Garantita) Very strictly controlled top quality Italian classification.

Dosage Adding of sweetened wine to disgorged bottles of champagne or sparkling wines made by *methode champenoise*.

Edelzwicker A term used in Alsace, meaning blends of more than one grape variety.

Eiswein Quality German wine made from grapes which were frozen during harvesting and pressing, usually very sweet.

Encepagement Grape variety used to produce the wine.

English Wine Wine produced from grapes grown in England.

Espalier system, high and low The training of vines on wires. The 'high' system refers to the Lenz Moser system as used in Austria and the 'low' system refers, for example, to the double guyot system as used in Bordeaux.

Flor A yeast that forms on the surface of wine maturing for fino sherry. It is an integral part of the development of the sherry.

Inlandische Schaumwein Sparkling wine made in Germany.

Kabinett The lowest grade for natural unsugared quality wine made in Germany.

Kakhetian method Fermentation of whole grapes in large earthenware vessels as used in Georgia.

Liebfraumilch A QbA wine (quality wine from a specified region) from Rheinhessen, Rheinpfalze, Nahe or Rheingau and made from specified grape varieties.

Macvin An aperitif from the Jura made from unfermented grape juice and brandy.

Mana system The cyprian version of the **Solera** system.

Methode Champenoise Sparkling wines made in the same way as champagne.

Moselblumchen A blended wine from the Mosel.

Mousseux Sparkling wine.

Perlwine German sparkling wine.

Petillant Slightly sparkling wine.

Phylloxera A parasitic insect, in leaf-eating or root-eating form, capable of destroying all European vines not grafted on to American root stock.

Pourriture gris, pourriture noble The *pourriture gris* or 'grey rot' is a type of grey mould that attacks grapes in cold wet conditions and ruins them. *Pourriture noble* or 'noble rot' is the same as **Botrytis Cinerea.**

QbA (Qualitätswein bestimmter Anbaugebiet) A quality wine from a designated region made in Germany.

QmP (Qualitätswein mit Prädikat) Top quality wine made in Germany.

RD (recently disgorged) Old champagne re-bottled before release on the market.

Remuage The regular twisting and turning of bottles to bring the sediment to the neck in the making of champagne. It can also refer to sparkling wines made by *methode champenoise*.

Rotling Light coloured red wine made in Germany.

Schaumwein Sparkling wine made in Germany.

Sekt A German-style sparkling wine.

Selection de grains nobles The Alsatian equivalent of the German Beerenauslese.

Solera system Used particularly in the making of sherry. Wines of the same quality and the same style are married together to produce a uniform blend of sherry.

Spätlese Quality German wine made from grapes left to ripen on the vine and harvested late.

Spitzenweine Wine from Spitz in Northern Austria.

Sur lie Wine that is bottled without being racked.

Tank method see **Charmat method or Cuvé Close.**

Trellis training system System of training vines above the ground.

Trockenbeeren auslese Quality German wine made from individual grapes affected by 'noble rot' and picked from selected bunches. See **Pourriture gris, Pourriture noble.**

Vendange tardive The French equivalent of the German Spätlese.

Vin delimité de Qualité Superieure (VDQS) The quality classification below Appellation Controlée in France.

Vin de comptoir Local wine sold in cafés in France.

Vin de pays Regional wine made in France.

Vin de paille Or 'vin jaune', a wine from the Jura made from grapes left on the vine to ripen late and then dried on straw mats.

Vin de table Table wine made in France.

Vin doux naturel Sweet wine made in France to which brandy has been added to stop fermentation and increase the alcohol content.

Vin gris A pink wine from Alsace.

Vin jaune see **Vin de paille.**

The Wine Index

Christopher Fielden's selection

To be asked to select one's 300 favourite wines poses a lot of
problems, but the following list is based soundly on tasting
notes I have made of well over 1,000 wines during the past
18 months. Because of my particular likes – and dislikes – it
tends to be somewhat unbalanced, with a greater proportion
of the wine coming from Burgundy and California. On the
other hand where I have tasted very little, I have included
some favourites of friends whose judgement I respect.

For the reason that they tend to be of standard quality, I
have not included champagnes and I would suggest that the
reader turns to page 49 for Pamela Vandyke Price's
appreciation of the different Houses.

This list reflects just one man's pleasure. It has been
compiled geographically by country, region and then
location.

What the entries mean

Name	The title of the wine as written on the label.
Vintage	A recent year that has produced a good wine. Other years are by no means ruled out.
Producer	The name of the wine producer as described on the label, not the importer.
Character	The editor's self-explanatory description of the wine.
Price	Four categories identify the range of price with * being the cheapest, or for everyday drinking, to ****.
Drink	An indicator as to when the wine should be drunk. o – should be drunk now oo – either drink now or keep for a while ooo – keep and drink later

BORDEAUX WHITE

Château Lauretan, Bordeaux blanc ✱✱ ○
1980 Clean. Pleasant grapey aftertaste

Château Bellevue, Graves de Vayres ✱✱ ○
1979 Dry, with crisp fruit

Château Lafaurie Peyraguey,
Sauternes ✱✱✱ ○○○
1980 A deep flavour of honey and lime. A great wine
for the future

Château Coutet, Barsac ✱✱✱ ○○
1976 Full, rich taste, with plenty of finesse

Château Liot, Barsac ✱✱✱ ○
1975 Creamy, luscious wine

BORDEAUX RED

Château Valrose, Bordeaux Supérieur ✱✱ ○○
1979 Medium body and long-lasting flavour

Château Patache d'Aux, Médoc ✱✱✱ ○○○
1978 Sound, full-bodied wine with plenty of future

Château la Cardonne, Médoc ✱✱✱ ○○
1976 Good fruit, agreeably soft, but with a hint of
tannin

Château Cissac, Médoc ✱✱✱ ○○
1976 Full-bodied and with a lot of flavour

Château Chasse-Spleen Moulis ✱✱✱ ○○
1976 Still restrained, will improve

Château Kirwan, Margaux ✱✱✱ ○○
1976 Elegant wine with some tannin still

Château Talbot, Saint Julien ✱✱✱ ○○○
1978 Very rich, but an iron fist in a velvet glove. A
long way to go

Château Gruaud-Larose, Saint Julien ✱✱✱✱ ○○○
1975 Full-bodied wine, with a very long future

Château Talbot, Saint Julien ✱✱✱✱ ○
1970 Rich, slightly burnt fruit taste; will improve

Château Grand Puy Ducasse, Pauillac ✱✱✱✱ ○○
1970 A great Médoc, with the body to support some
more ageing

Château Latour, Pauillac ✱✱✱✱ ○○○
1978 Young looking, complex flavours; the tannin to
support a long life

Château La Tour Haut Vignoble,
Saint Estèphe ✱✱✱ ○○
1975 Deep restrained wine, not yet at its best

Château Meyney, Saint Estèphe ✱✱✱ ○○
1976 Deep coloured wine, with rich appley taste

Domaine de Chevalier, Graves ✱✱✱ ○
1973 Very appealing claret, with plenty of fruit

Vieux Château Certan, Pomerol ✱✱✱ ○○
1976 Soft, rich wine. Most agreeable

Château Fombrauge, Saint Emilion ✱✱✱ ○○○
   1975   Great wine with full-bodied fruit
Château Clos des Jacobins, Saint Emilion ✱✱✱ ○○○
   1978   Big and round, should be an enjoyable wine for a
long time

BURGUNDY WHITE
Sauvignon de Saint Bris ✱✱ ○
   1978   Michel Rémon   Agreeable, dry fruitiness
Chablis Domaine des Valéry ✱✱ ○○
   1979   Durup   Very big nose and flavour
Chablis ✱✱ ○○
   1978   A Regnard et Fils   Full-bodied, pleasant drinking
Chablis 1er cru Mont de Milieu ✱✱ ○○○
   1979   Bacheroy-Josselin   Rich, full of flavour. Well-
balanced wine with some acidity
Chablis 1er cru Vaillons ✱✱ ○○
   1979   Domaine la Jouchère   Agreeable, well-balanced
wine
Chablis les Clos ✱✱✱ ○○○
   1981   Joseph Drouhin   Big wine with a long way to go
Chablis les Clos ✱✱✱ ○○○
   1978   Joseph Drouhin   Rich and full-bodied
Chablis Vaudesir ✱✱✱ ○○
   1979   Prosper Maufoux   Delicate, exotic fruit flavour,
very pleasant
Corton Charlemagne ✱✱✱ ○○
   1980   Bonneau de Martray   A great wine from a lesser
vintage
Corton Charlemagne ✱✱✱✱ ○○○
   1979   Louis Jadot   Full-bodied, earthy start, with
beautiful finish
Corton Charlemagne ✱✱✱✱ ○
   1975   Bonneau de Martray   A great wine at its peak
Pernand Vergelesses ✱✱ ○○
   1979   François Germain   Crisp, with plenty of fruit
Beaune Clos des Mouches ✱✱✱ ○○
   1978   Joseph Drouhin   Full, big nose. Well balanced
with plenty of finesse
Meursault 1er cru ✱✱✱ ○
   1973   Gauffroy   A class wine with a lot of finesse
Meursault Charmes Hospices de Beaune Cuvée
  A. Grivault ✱✱✱✱ ○○○
   1979   Prosper Maufoux   Typical nutty flavour
Meursault Charmes ✱✱✱ ○
   1977   Domaine Monnier   Good, full flavour
Meursault Perrières ✱✱✱ ○○○
   1979   Ropiteau-Mignon   Gentle start, but enormous
Meursault finish
Meursault Poruzots Medaille d'argent ✱✱✱ ○○
   1979   Henri de Villamont   Fine acidity, nutty fullness

Meursault Poruzots *** o
  1973   Caves de la Reine Pedauque   Not very Meursault
  on nose but typical on palate. A great deal of charm
Puligny Montrachet *** oo
  1979   Louis Jadot   Beautiful, delicate finesse
Puligny Montrachet *** oo
  1978   Louis Latour   A great, full-bodied white
  Burgundy
Puligny Chalumeaux *** oo
  1979   Ropiteau–Mignon   Delicate wine, with a lot of
  finesse
Puligny Montrachet Folatières *** oo
  1979   Prosper Maufoux   Exquisite delicacy of flavour
Puligny Montrachet les Perrières *** o
  1977   Etienne Sauzet   Perfect light, but concentrated
  taste
Chevalier Montrachet **** ooo
  1979   Prosper Maufoux   Superb, will age well
le Montrachet **** ooo
  1979   Marquis de Laguiche   Fantastic depth with very
  complex flavours
Chassagne Montrachet *** oo
  1978   Morey   Interesting wine with deep taste
Chassagne Montrachet la Boudriotte *** oo
  1978   Gagnard-Delagrange   Full-bodied, with intense
  chardonnay flavour
Chassagne Montrachet Caillerets *** oo
  1978   Jean-Noel Gagnard   Excellent wine with plenty
  of body
Chassagne Montrachet Morgeot *** oo
  1978   Morey   Very good and will improve
Santenay Clos des Gravières *** oo
  1979   Prosper Maufoux   Excellent fruity nose, round
  and full-bodied
Rully Varots ** oo
  1980   Domaine de la Renarde   Fruity, crisp chardonnay
Montagny ler cru ** oo
  1979   Guyot   Very clean and refreshing
Macon Chardonnay Medaille d'Or ** o
  1979   CCMC   Crisp wine with well-balanced acidity
Macon Supérieur ** o
  1978   Cave Cooperative de Buxy   Good, clean nose.
  Slightly spicy taste
Beaujolais Blanc ** o
  1978   Louis Jadot   Full nose and flavour
Saint Véran ** o
  1980   Desvignes Ainé   Light and refreshing
Saint Véran ** o
  1980   UCVB   Agreeable, fruity chardonnay
Pouilly Fuisse, Ch. de Fuissé *** oo
  1977   Deep, dry and rather austere

BURGUNDY RED

Bourgogne Passetousgrains ** ○
1978 Clair-Däu Fresh, easy drinking basic Burgundy

Bourgogne ** ○
1979 E. Loron et Fils. Well-balanced, fruity wine

Bourgogne Cuvée Alexis Chanson ** ○○
1976 Chanson Père et Fils Good pinot nose. Some tannin, will last well

Bourgogne Irancy, Pinot Noir ** ○○
1979 Bacheroy-Josselin Well balanced, with some depth

Bourgogne Hautes Côtes de Beaune Médaille d'Or ** ○○
1979 Mazilly Père et Fils Fresh, pleasant pinot flavour

Bourgogne de Marsannay **
1978 Clair-Däu Classic, simple pinot noir

Côte de Nuits Villages ** ○
1977 Naudin Good, simple, easy-drinking wine

Gevrey-Chambertin *** ○○
1980 Joseph Drouhin Good colour and flavour; a little tannin

Gevrey-Chambertin les Champeaux *** ○○
1972 Leroy Rich and full tasting

Gevrey-Chambertin Clos du Chapitre *** ○○○
1978 Henri de Villamon Big-bodied wine with tannin

Charmes-Chambertin **** ○○○
1978 Prosper Maufoux A lot of finesse and body. Will be excellent

Bonnes Mares **** ○○○
1978 Prosper Maufoux Superb deep flavour

Bonnes Mares **** ○
1970 Chanson Père et Fils Excellent rich old wine

Chambolle-Musigny Charmes *** ○○○
1978 Michel Clerget Tight wine, opening out to full raspberry taste

le Musigny *** ○○
1972 de Vogüé A beautiful wine, not yet at its best

Vougeot Clos de la Perrière **** ○○
1966 Bertagna Excellent full-bodied wine with plenty of flavour

Grands Echézeaux **** ○○
1977 Chanson Père et Fils Fine, rich Côte de Nuits

Grands Echézeaux **** ○○
1969 Domaine de la Romanée Conti Full-bodied and deep character

Vosne Romanée *** ○○○
1976 Remoissenet Plenty of depth, will make a very agreeable bottle

Vosne Romanée Chaumes *** ○○○
1978 Prosper Maufoux Slightly soft, full fruit a delightful wine

Vosne Romanée Malconsorts **** OOO
  1976 Moillard Full-bodied, with some tannin. Fine flavour in the background
Vosne Romanée les Violettes *** OO
  1978 Georges Clerget Rich restrained taste
Nuits Saint Georges les Boudots *** OOO
  1976 Prosper Maufoux Top-quality flavour. A long way to go
Nuits Saint Georges Damodes *** OO
  1978 Machard de Gramont Deep, full flavoured, but forward
Nuits Saint Georges les Saint Georges Hospices de Nuits, Cuvée des Sires de Vergy **** OOO
  1978 J.-C. Boisset Good, deep-bodied pinot, with plenty of fruit
Côte de Beaune Villages ** OO
  1978 Louis Jadot Some tannin, should mature well
Aloxe Corton *** O
  1978 Louis Jadot Soft start, but a lot of body
Corton **** OOO
  1979 Louis Jadot A great mouthful of fine Burgundy
Corton *** OO
  1977 Tollot Beaut A soft full-flavoured wine from an unfashionable vintage
Corton Bressandes **** O
  1962 Caves de la Reine Pedauque Full, rich silk
Corton Clos de la Vigne au Saint **** OOO
  1978 Prosper Maufoux Beautiful nose, rich body, long way to go
Pernand Vergelesses les Vergelesses *** OO
  1979 Chanson Père et Fils Delicate finesse
Chorey les Beaune ** OO
  1978 Joseph Drouhin Excellent young pinot characteristics
Savigny Clos des Guettes *** OO
  1978 Henri de Villamont Rich colour, good pinot nose. Full body, soft but tannic
Beaune Clos des Fèves *** OOO
  1977 Chanson Père et Fils Deep and tannic, a wine for the future
Beaune Clos des Fèves *** OO
  1972 Chanson Père et Fils Rich, full, fruity flavour
Beaune Grèves *** OOO
  1976 Moillard Good, big and rich. Stacks of tannin
Beaune Grèves *** O
  1972 Albert Morey A good balance between fruit and body
Beaune Grèves *** OO
  1969 Paul Chanson A sleeping giant
Beaune Clos des Marconnets *** OO
  1977 Chanson Père et Fils Opening out into a great wine

Beaune Clos des Mouches ✳✳✳ ○○
1979 Chanson Père et Fils Fruity, soft and enjoyable
Beaune Clos des Mouches ✳✳✳ ○○
1979 Joseph Drouhin Very elegant and silky
Beaune Teurons ✳✳✳ ○○
1978 Chanson Père et Fils Full-bodied, with plenty of fruit
Beaune Teurons ✳✳✳ ○○
1976 Bouchard Père et Fils Rich and stout; surprisingly far advanced
Beaune Teurons ✳✳✳ ○○○
1972 Leroy Still tight, but should open out into something great
Beaune Theurons ✳✳✳ ○○
1979 Louis Jadot Very elegant and flavoursome
Beaune Theurons ✳✳✳ ○○○
1976 Louis Jadot Soft and rich; well balanced, with some tannin
Beaune Clos des Ursules ✳✳✳ ○○○
1979 Louis Jadot Full-bodied, blackcurrant finish
Pommard ✳✳✳ ○○○
1978 Chanson Père et Fils Meaty wine with a long way to go
Volnay Clos des Chênes ✳✳✳✳ ○○
1962 Leroy Smooth, soft and full of fruit
Volnay Chevrets ✳✳✳ ○○
1980 Prosper Maufoux An agreeable light wine with delicate pinot flavour
Santenay Saint Michel ✳✳ ○○○
1978 Prosper Maufoux Very deep colour. Taste of fresh red fruits. Some tannin
Mercurey ✳✳ ○○○
1978 Prosper Maufoux Dull nose; tight with enormous body. Will become something very good
Mercurey ✳✳ ○○○
1978 Domaine de la Renarde Full bodied, attractive wine
Rully ✳✳ ○○
1979 Domaine de la Renarde Soft fruity, easy drinking wine
Givry ✳✳ ○○
1980 Joseph Drouhin Rich, flavoursome, soft swigger
Givry Clos du Cellier aux Moines ✳✳ ○○
1979 Delorme Deep-coloured, rich flavour

BEAUJOLAIS
Mâcon Rouge ✳✳ ○
1979 L'Eventail Good Gamay nose; pleasant, fresh wine
Beaujolais Villages Bérangère ✳✳ ○
1981 Pasquier-Desvignes Fruity, easy-drinking wine

Beaujolais Villages, Domaine de la Maison Rouge ** ○
1980 Henri de Villamont Excellent colour and depth
Beaujolais Villages Chêne ** ○
1981 André Jaffre Rich enjoyable raspberry taste
Brouilly ** ○
1979 Prosper Maufoux Soft nose and a surprising amount of body after an easy start
Brouilly Domaine Combillaty ** ○
1976 Georges Duboeuf Fruity wine, now at its peak
Morgon Domaine Saint Joseph ** ○
1978 Pellerin Soft and full-bodied
Morgon Cuvée Jean Descombes ** ○
1976 Georges Duboeuf Flatteringly rich
Chiroubles ** ○
1979 Louis Jadot Fairly deep with a little tannin
Chiroubles ** ○
1979 Desvignes Aîné Easy, pleasant drinking
Saint Armour ** ○
1978 Prosper Maufoux Beautiful, rich, silky wine
Moulin à Vent Domaine Granger ** ○○○
1980 Desvignes Aîné Rich colour, deep, restrained flavour
Moulin à Vent *** ○○
1976 Pasquier-Desvignes Deep and full-bodied. A fine Beaujolais

ALSACE

Edelzwicker d'Alsace ** ○
1979 Cave Coopérative de Kientzheim Good, basic, clean Alsace
Pinot Blanc ** ○
1979 A. Willm Very good, light fruity wine
Riesling, Cuvée des Ecaillers ** ○
1979 Léon Beyer Clean, crisp varietal flavour
Gewurztraminer ** ○
1978 Léon Beyer Fine and flavoursome
Gewurztraminer Clos Saint Landelin ** ○○
1978 A. & O. Mure Clean, crisp and full of fruit
Gewurztraminer Kaefferkopf Gold Medal ** ○○
1979 Cave Coopérative de Kientzheim Beautiful, well balanced, very spicy
Gewurztztraminer Eichberg Vendange Tardive Reserve Speciale *** ○○
1976 Dopff 'au Moulin' Outstanding, full-bodied flavour
Gewurztraminer Vendange Tardive, Selectionné par Jean Hugel **** ○○
1976 F. E. Hugel Fine, rich wine

SPARKLING WINES

Hochriegl Alte Reserve ** O
Johann Kattus-Vienna   Very clean and light

Vouvray Pétillant ** O
1978   Marc Brédif   Delightful, fresh wine

Saumur Brut de Blanc ** O
Bouvet-Ladubay   Very crisp

Fleur de Lys Blanquette de Limoux ** O
1978   Full-bodied, dry and refreshing

RHONE WHITE

Côtes du Ventoux ** O
1980   Picard Père et Fils   Soft, easy drinking

St. Péray ** OO
1980   Delas   Full-bodied and dry. A big mouthful

Crozes Hermitage ** OO
1978   Caves de la Reine Pédauque   Herbal nose; a
round and heavy wine

Viognier, Condrieu Château du Rozay *** OOO
1980   Paul Multier   Dry, but at the same time rich.
Highly flavoured. Characteristics of the grape

Muscat de Beaumes de Venise.
Domaine de Durban *** O
1977   Jacques Leydier   One of the great sweet wines of
France. Grapey

RHONE ROSE

Côtes du Rhône Chusclan Seigneurie de Gicon ** O
1980   Cave Coopérative de Chusclan   Soft, pleasant full

RHONE RED

Vin de Pays de Gamay de l'Ardêche ** O
1980   Cave Coopérative de Saint Désirat Champagne
Fruity, Gamay flavour. An easy wine to drink

Côteaux du Tricastin; Cru de Méynas ** OOO
1978   Pierre Labeye   Rich, full-bodied and tannic

Côtes du Rhône Tournoi ** O
1980   Pasquier Desvignes   Good, hearty, basic Côtes du
Rhône

Gigondas Domaine Saint Guyon ** OO
1978   Roger Meffre   Superb, quality Rhône wine

Vacqueyras ** O
1977   Picard Père et Fils   Deep-coloured, very full-
bodied, rich taste

Lirac Domaine de Castel Oualou ** O
1976   Pons-Mure   Deep, heady wine

Côte Rotie, la Chevaliere d'Ampuis *** OOO
1978   Robert Jasmin   Deep, heavy and rich, will make
a very great wine

Hermitage *** OOO
1978   Gereard Cave   Intense body; a long way to go

Hermitage **** ooo
1962   Délépine   Full round wine, with plenty of meat
Châteauneuf du Pape; Château de Thabor *** oo
1978   Henri de Villamont   Deep violet colour,
strapping wine, full of tannin
**Châteauneuf du Pape Domaine
de la Solitude** ** oo
1967   A robust mouthful with still some future. An old-
fashioned Châteauneuf du Pape

LOIRE
**Muscadet de Sèvre et Maine, Château de Cléray,
sur lie** ** o
1981   Crisp and dry
Sauvignon de Haut Poitou * o
1980   Cave Coopérative de Haut Poitou   Very clean,
fresh flavour
Saumur Blanc ** o
1981   Cave de Saint-Cyr   Rather acid start, but very
refreshing
Vouvray, Demi-sec *** oo
1978   Marc Brédif   Magnificent, full flavour with clean
sweetness
Malvoisie, Ancénis ** o
1978   Jacques Guindon   Rich and clean, with definitely
sweet undertones
Blanc Fumé de Pouilly ** o
1979   Prosper Maufoux   Soft and agreeable; goes well
Blanc Fumé de Pouilly ** o
1979   G. Coulbois   Pleasant, clean wine with finesse
Sancerre ** o
1981   Pierre Riffault   Full-bodied, but not aggressive
Sauvignon

SOUTH OF FRANCE WHITE
**Domaine de Gourgazaud
Vin de Pays de l'Hérault** ** o
Gourgazaud   Fresh, well-balanced wine
Sauvignon, Vin de Pays de l'Oc ** o
Salins du Midi   Crisp wine with the true Sauvignon taste
**Blanc de Blancs, Vin de Pays des Sables du Golfe du
Lyons** ** o
Salins du Midi   Clean and refreshing

SOUTH OF FRANCE RED
Minervois la Livinière ** oo
1979   Demolombe   Excellent grapey nose, good
drinking now, but will keep
Minervois Cuvée Jean d'Alibert ** oo
1978   SICA Vigneronne et Vinicole de Peyriac   Full-
bodied, with deep flavour

Minervois Château de Gourgazaud ** ○○
   1979   A great deal of breeding, enhanced by ageing in
oak casks
Corbières Château les Palais ** ○○○
   1979   Demolombe   Very deep colour; excellent, full,
rich restrained wine with a long way to go
Cahors Domaine de Menguet ** ○○○
   1978   Menguet   A sound, intense wine for the future

GERMAN WINES
MOSEL
Ayler Kupp Riesling Spätlese ** ○
   1979   Winzerverein Ayl   Light delicate wine for
summer drinking
Bernkasteler Doktor Riesling Spätlese *** ○
   1976   Deinhard   Very elegant
Serriger Herrenberg Riesling Auslese *** ○
   1978   Bert Simon   Gracious wine with a great finesse
Piesporter Gunterslay Auslese *** ○
   1975   Ulrich Langguth   Delicious wine with fresh
sweetness
RHEINGAU
Hattenheimer Deutelsberg ** ○
   1979   Hans Lang   Soft, fruity and full of flavour
Rauenthaler Steinmächer Riesling Kabinett *** ○
   1979   Schloss Schönborn   Elegant, full-bodied wine
Hochheimer Königin Victoria Berg, Spätlese *** ○
   1975   Königin   Deep round full nose and body. Very
big wine
**Hochheimer Königin Victoria Berg
Beerenauslese** *** ○○
   1976   Königin   Enormous mouthful of beautiful flavour
NAHE
**Kreuznacher Himmelgarten Müller-Thurgau Halb
Trocken** ** ○
   1978   Simmerner hof   Fruity wine with a little
sweetness. Easy drinking
PALATINATE
Ruppertsberger Geiseböhl Spätlese *** ○○
   1978   Dr. Bürklin-Wolff   Full, rich flavour
**Wachenheimer Rechbachel Riesling
Kabinett** *** ○
   1975   Dr. Bürklin-Wolff   Rich, fruity Palatinate wine
at its best

ITALIAN WINE
Galestro ** ○
   1980   Antinori   Very crisp and fresh, with a lot of fruit
Soave Classico ** ○
   1980   Pieropan   Clean and full of flavour

ITALIAN RED
Costa della Pergole ** ooo
1978   Col Sandigo   Good, deep colour. Full-bodied, classy, Bordeaux style
Ghiaie della Furba Tenuta di Capezzana ** oo
1979   Contini Bonacossi   Full colour, well-balanced wine with tannin
Rubesco Torgiano ** o
1974   Lungarotti   Quality soft red wine
Tignanello *** oo
1971   Antinori   Fine mature wine, showing the benefit of cask ageing
Sassicaia *** o
1975   Antinori   A classical wine from the Cabernet grape
Chianti Classico Castell'in Villa ** oo
1977   Principessa Pignatelli   Excellent wine with a lot of fruit
Barolo *** ooo
1975   Pio Cesare   Old style meaty Barolo
Brunello di Montalcino **** ooo
1975   Col d'Orcia   Corpulent red, needs opening well before drinking

SPAIN WHITE
Blanc de Blancs * o
Marqués de Monistrol   Very clean and crisp
Gran Viña Sol 'Green Label' ** o
1978   Torres   Full-bodied wine, with plenty of flavour on the nose and palate
Marqués de Cáceres, Rioja ** oo
1981   Unión Viti-Vinícola   Full, dry wine with great intensity of flavour

SPAIN RED
Gran Coronas *** oo
1975   Torres   Wxceptionally deep wine with a way to go
Lan Rioja ** o
1976   Bodegas Lan   Well-balanced, agreeable wine
Marqués de Cáceres, Rioja ** oo
1976   Unión Viti-Vinícola   Full, round flavour; very long in the mouth
Viña Salceda Rioja *** o
1975   Viña Salceda   Light with finesse; long finish
Marqués de Cáceres Reserva Rioja *** oo
1970   Unión Viti-Vinícola   Great wine which will last
Viña Salceda Reserva Rioja *** oo
1970   Viña Salceda   Full-bodied, heavy wine
Vega Sicilia **** ooo
1967   Vega Sicilia   Enormous brute of a wine which will last for (almost) ever

PORTUGAL
Alvarinho, Vinho Verde ⋆⋆⋆ ○
1979 Palacio da Brejoeira An incredible, full-bodied complex wine

CALIFORNIA WHITE
Premium White ⋆⋆ ○
Fetzer Vineyards Complex and full of flavour
Californian Dry White ⋆ ○
Guimarra Clean, fruity wine
Californian White ⋆ ○
Paul Masson Simple, fresh drinking
Beaufort Pinot Chardonnay, Napa ⋆⋆⋆ ○
1979 Beaulieu Vineyards Good finesse, well balanced
Chardonnay, Napa Valley ⋆⋆⋆ ○○
1979 Burgess Cellars Full-bodied and round; good varietal flavour
Chardonnay, Napa ⋆⋆⋆ ○○
1978 Conn Creek Vineyard Crisp wine with full body
Chardonnay, Santa Ynez ⋆⋆⋆ ○○
1980 Firestone Vineyard Rich and full tasting
Chardonnay, Monterey ⋆⋆⋆ ○○
1980 Jekel Vineyards Intense chardonnay flavour, with hint of oak
Chardonnay, Napa ⋆⋆⋆ ○○
1980 Robert Mondavi Rich and round, a huge mouthful
Chardonnay, Napa ⋆⋆⋆ ○○
1979 Trefethen Vineyards Clean and crisp, with lingering traces of oak
Chardonnay Napa ⋆⋆⋆ ○
1977 Trefethen Vineyards Excellent finesse and length of flavour
Chardonnay, Belle Terre ⋆⋆⋆⋆ ○○○
1980 Château Saint Jean Big wine with well-balanced acidity
Chardonnay, Alexander Valley ⋆⋆⋆ ○○
1978 Sausal Winery Melon taste, attractive, but different!
Chardonnay, Santa Ynez ⋆⋆⋆ ○○
1979 Zaca Mesa Winery Full and round, with well-balanced acidity. Good varietal characteristic
Chenin Blanc Sonoma ⋆⋆ ○
1978 Pedroncelli Vineyards Interesting, full flavour
Colombard ⋆⋆ ○
1979 Stone Creek Vineyards Agreeable, full-bodied wine
Fumé Blanc, Sonoma ⋆⋆⋆ ○
1980 Dry Creek Vineyards Crisp, assertive, Sauvignon taste

Fumé Blanc, Napa *** ○○
1980   Robert Mondavi   Full-bodied, clean, rich wine
Gewurztraminer *** ○
1979   Fetzer Vineyards   Excellent varietal characteristic
Gewurztraminer Santa Ynez *** ○
1979   Firestone Vineyard   Fruity and spicy
Gewurztraminer Napa Valley
   Centennial Vintage *** ○
1979   Inglenook Vineyards   Fresh and flavoursome
Gewurztraminer Belle Terre Vineyards Alexander
   Valley; Individual bunch selected late harvest
   **** ○○○
1978   Château Saint Jean   Complicated heaveyweight,
with rich spiciness
Moscato d'Oro Napa *** ○
1980   Robert Mondavi   Clean, rich dessert wine
Johannisberg Riesling, Ambassador's Vineyard,
   Santa Ynez *** ○
1978   Firestone Vineyard   Full of flavour
Johannisberg Riesling Ambassador's Vineyard,
   Selected Harvest, Santa Ynez **** ○○○
1978   Firestone Vineyard   Rich, smooth and honied
Riesling, Late harvest, Monterey **** ○○○
1980   Jekel Vineyards   Intense, rich flavour with
balancing acidity; a great wine
Riesling, Napa County *** ○
1978   Markham Winery   Very fruity, full-bodied wine
White Riesling, Napa *** ○
1979   Trefethen Vineyards   Very good, clean flavour

CALIFORNIA RED
Californian Red * ○
Paul Masson   Good, solid fruit. Uncomplicated
Premium Red; Mendocino ** ○
Fetzer Vineyards   Deep rich many-stranded flavour
Cabernet Sauvignon Vintage Selection
   Napa *** ○○
1977   Burgess Cellars   Rich, intense and tannic
Cabernet Sauvignon; Santa Ynez *** ○○○
1977   Firestone Vineyard   Big and robust
Cabernet Sauvignon; Martha's Vineyard,
   Napa **** ○○○
1976   Heitz Cellars   Big, herbal, tannic wine
Cabernet Sauvignon, Sonoma *** ○○○
1978   Iron Horse   Well balanced, long-lasting, with
plenty of tannin
Cabernet Sauvignon, Private Reserve,
   Monterey **** ○○○
1978   Jekel Vineyards   Great, tannic wine. Rich and
restrained; a long way to go

Cabernet Sauvignon, Napa *** OO
1977 Robert Mondavi Elegant wine with finesse
Cabernet Sauvignon, Napa *** OO
1978 Trefethen Vineyards Varietal flavour with breeding
Cabernet Sauvignon, Napa *** OO
1976 Trefethen Vineyards Rich, full-bodied wine
Merlot Sonoma *** OO
1978 Clos du Bois Mellow class
Merlot, Napa *** OO
1978 Clos du Val Beautiful, soft and elegant
Merlot, Ambassador's Vineyard, Santa Ynez *** OO
1978 Firestone Vineyard Big, rich and soft
Merlot, Ambassador's Vineyard, Santa Ynez *** OO
Pinot Noir, Napa County *** OO
1978 Carneros Creek Full varietal flavour, with oaky background
Pinot Noir, Santa Ynez *** O
1975 Firestone Vineyard Soft style of great Burgundy
Pinot Noir, Santa Barbara *** OOO
1978 Trefethen Vineyards Sappy, grape character
Petite Syrah Mendocino ** OO
1977 Fetzer Vineyards Fruity, deep-coloured wine
Syrah, Napa *** OOO
1977 Joseph Phelps Vineyard Rich and tannic
Zinfandel, Napa *** OO
1977 Caymus Vineyards Soft, but with a lot of tannin in the background
Zinfandel, Napa *** OO
1976 Cuvaison Full-bodied and meaty
Zinfandel, Sonoma *** OO
1977 Kenwood Slight nose. Lots of finesse at start, tannic
Zinfandel, Late Harvest, Napa *** OOO
1978 Mayacamas Vineyards Rich and tannic; needs to age seriously
Zinfandel Mendocino ** OOO
1979 Parducci Wine Cellars Very tannic, thin front, but good follow-up
Zinfandel, Alameda *** O
1977 Pendleton Winery Deep, with a lot of finesse. Apparently made from very old vines
Zinfandel *** OOO
1978 Ridge Vineyards Slightly stalky, but with a lot of flavour and tannin
Zinfandel, Paso Robles *** OO
1979 Ridge Vineyards Soft and full-bodied
Zinfandel, Late Harvest, Napa *** OOO
1978 Rutherford Ranch Cellars Big, heavy, rich wine with a dryish finish

AUSTRALIA RED
Cabernet Sauvignon, Coonawarra ✳✳✳ OO
   1977   Wynn's   Excellent Cabernet by any standards
Cabernet Sauvignon, Victoria ✳✳✳ OOO
   1978   Taltarni Vineyards   Full-bodied wine with plenty
   of tannin and oak
Château Clare Cabernet Sauvignon ✳✳✳ OO
   1977   Taylor's   Deep, complex bouquet with full body
Shiraz Coonawarra ✳✳✳ OOO
   1977   Redman's   Flower bouquet; deep tannic wine

SOUTH AFRICA WHITE
Paarl Riesling Paarl ✳✳ O
   1980   Nederburg   Full-bodied and rich
Fonternel Coastal Region ✳✳ O
   1980   Nederburg   Flowery nose, slightly sweet populist
   taste
Fleur Du Cap Chenin Blanc Sec ✳✳ O
   1981   Bergkelder   Dry well-balanced fruity wine

SOUTH AFRICA RED
Baronne Coastal Region ✳✳ OO
   1977   Nederburg   Deep flavour, with some tannin
Cabernet Sauvignon, Paarl ✳✳ OOO
   1978   Nederburg   Heavy, full-bodied varietal wine
Jacobsdal Pinotage ✳✳✳ O
   1976   Jacobsdal   Smooth and full-flavoured
Alles Verooren Tinta, Barocca ✳✳ OOO
   1978   Alles Verooren   Rich, robust wine

AUSTRIA
Ruster St. Georgen Gewurztraminer ✳✳ O
   1978   Sepp-Hold   Excellent, clean varietal characteristic
Rust Neusiedlersee Muskat-Ottonel ✳✳ O
   1979   Herrenhaus Kellerei   Good, delicate fruity flavour
Gewurztraminer ✳✳ O
   1979   Schlosskellerei Uhlheim   Light and fragrant

SWITZERLAND
Domaine de Autecour ✳✳✳ O
   1973   Obrist   Very fruity exotic taste of old sweet wine
Domaine de Autecour ✳✳✳ O
   1971   Obrist   Initial taste of old Sauternes. Very long in
   the mouth
Muscat Molignon Cuvée Speciale ✳✳✳ OO
   1980   Maurice Gay   Enormous grape flavour with light,
   clean finish
Mont d'Or Hermitage ✳✳✳ OOO
   1980   Mont d'Or   Strawberry nose, rich fruit flavour;
   very long lasting on the palate